On
Belief

Praise for the series

'. . . allows a space for distinguished thinkers to write about their passions.'
The Philosophers' Magazine

'. . . deserve high praise.'
Boyd Tonkin, The Independent (UK)

'This is clearly an important series. I look forward to reading future volumes.'
Frank Kermode, author of Shakespeare's Language

'. . . both rigorous and accessible.'
Humanist News

'. . . the series looks superb.'
Quentin Skinner

'. . . an excellent and beautiful series.'
Ben Rogers, author of A.J. Ayer: A Life

'Routledge's *Thinking in Action* series is the theory junkie's answer to the eminently pocketable Penguin 60s series.'
Mute Magazine (UK)

'Routledge's new series, *Thinking in Action*, brings philosophers to our aid . . .'
The Evening Standard (UK)

'. . . a welcome new series by Routledge.'
Bulletin of Science, Technology and Society (Can)

SLAVOJ ŽIŽEK

On
Belief

Routledge
Taylor & Francis Group

LONDON AND NEW YORK

First published 2001
by Routledge
2 Park Square, Milton Park, Abingdon, Oxon, OX14 4RN

Simultaneously published in the USA and Canada
by Routledge
270 Madison Ave, New York, NY 10016

Reprinted 2002 (twice), 2003 (twice), 2004, 2005, 2006, 2007 (twice)

Transferred to Digital Printing 2009

Routledge is an imprint of the Taylor & Francis Group, an informa business

© 2001 Slavoj Žižek

Typeset in Joanna MT by
RefineCatch Limited, Bungay, Suffolk
Printed and bound in Great Britain by
TJI Digital, Padstow, Cornwall

All rights reserved. No part of this book may be reprinted or
reproduced or utilised in any form or by any electronic,
mechanical, or other means, now known or hereafter
invented, including photocopying and recording, or in any
information storage or retrieval system, without permission in
writing from the publishers.

British Library Cataloguing in Publication Data
A catalogue record for this book is available from the British Library

Library of Congress Cataloging in Publication Data
Žižek, Slavoj
    On belief / Slavoj Žižek.
      p. cm. – (Thinking in action)
    Includes index.
    1. Belief and doubt. 2. Faith. I. Title. II. Series.
  BD215 .Z59 2001
  291.2 – dc21   00–065336

ISBN10: 0–415–25531–7 (hbk)
ISBN10: 0–415–25532–5 (pbk)
ISBN13: 978–0–415–25531–8 (hbk)
ISBN13: 978–0–415–25532–5 (pbk)

Mixed Sources
Product group from well-managed
forests and other controlled sources
www.fsc.org Cert no. SGS-COC-2482
© 1996 Forest Stewardship Council
FSC

Introduction: From Christ to Lenin . . . and Back   1

Against the Digital Heresy   One   6

Gnosticism? No, Thanks!   6
From the Thing to Objects a . . . and Back   15
No Sex, Please, We're Digital!   33
The Antinomy of Cyberspace Reason   48

You *Should* Give a Shit!   Two   56

The Anal Object   56
Sacrifice versus the Feminine Renunciation   68
The Real of the (Christian) Illusion   79
God Resides in Details   89

"Father, Why Did You Forsake Me?"   Three   106

Faith Without Belief   109
The Leninist Freedom   113
Why the Jewish Iconoclasm?   127
Author, Subject, Executioner   137
No Mercy!   142

Notes   152
Index   166

Introduction: From Christ to Lenin . . . and Back

In the Larry King debate between a rabbi, a Catholic priest and a Southern Baptist, broadcast in March 2000, both the rabbi and the priest expressed their hope that the unification of religions is feasible since, irrespective of his or her official creed, a thoroughly good person can count on divine grace and redemption. Only the Baptist – a young, well-tanned, slightly overweight and repulsively slick Southern yuppie – insisted that, according to the letter of the Gospel, only those who "live in Christ" by explicitly recognizing themselves in his address will be redeemed, which is why, as he concluded with a barely discernible contemptuous smile, "a lot of good and honest people will burn in hell." In short, goodness (applying common moral norms) which is not directly grounded in the Gospel is ultimately just a perfidious semblance of itself, its own travesty . . . The basic premise of this book[1] is that, cruel as this position may sound, if one is to break the liberal–democratic hegemony and resuscitate an authentic radical position, one has to endorse its materialist version. IS there such a version?

Today, even self-proclaimed post-Marxist radicals endorse the gap between ethics and politics, relegating politics to the domain of *doxa*, of pragmatic considerations and compromises which always and by definition fall short of the unconditional ethical demand. The notion of a politics which would not

1 **On** Belief

have been a series of mere pragmatic interventions, but the politics of Truth, is dismissed as "totalitarian." The breaking out of this deadlock, the reassertion of a politics of Truth today, should take the form of a *return to Lenin*. Why Lenin, why not simply Marx? Is the proper return not the return to origins proper? Today, "returning to Marx" is already a minor academic fashion. *Which* Marx do we get in these returns? On the one hand, the Cultural Studies Marx, the Marx of the postmodern sophists, of the Messianic promise; on the other hand, the Marx who foretold the dynamic of today's globalization and is as such evoked even on Wall Street. What both these Marxes have in common is the *denial of politics proper*; the reference to Lenin enables us to avoid these two pitfalls.

There are two features which distinguish his intervention. First, one cannot emphasize enough the fact of Lenin's *externality* with regard to Marx: he was not a member of Marx's "inner circle" of the initiated, he never met either Marx or Engels; moreover, he came from a land at the Eastern borders of "European civilization." (This externality is part of the standard Western racist argument against Lenin: he introduced into Marxism the Russian–Asiatic "despotic principle"; in one remove further, Russians themselves disown him, pointing towards his Tatar origins.) It is only possible to retrieve the theory's original impulse from this external position; in exactly the same way St Paul, who formulated the basic tenets of Christianity, was not part of Christ's inner circle, and Lacan accomplished his "return to Freud" using a totally distinct theoretical tradition as a leverage. (Freud was aware of this necessity, which is why he put his trust in a non-Jew, and outsider – Jung – to break out of this closed circle of a community based on initiation through wisdom. However, his choice was a poor one, because Jungian theory itself functions as wisdom based on initiation; it was Lacan who succeeded where Jung failed.) So, in the same way that St Paul and Lacan reinscribe the original teaching into a different context (St Paul reinterprets Christ's crucifixion as his triumph; Lacan reads Freud through the mirror-stage Saussure), Lenin violently displaces Marx, tears his theory out of its original context, planting it in another historical moment, and thus effectively universalizes it.

Second, it is only through such a violent displacement that the "original" theory can be put to work, fulfilling its potential of political intervention. It is significant that the work in which Lenin's unique voice was for the first time clearly heard is *What Is To Be Done?* – the text which exhibits Lenin's unconditional will to intervene into the situation, not in the pragmatic sense of "adjusting the theory to the realistic claims through necessary compromises," but, on the contrary, in the sense of dispelling all opportunistic compromises, of adopting the unequivocal radical position from which it is only possible to intervene in such a way that our intervention changes the coordinates of the situation. The contrast is here clear with regard to today's Third Way "postpolitics," which emphasizes the need to leave behind old ideological divisions and to confront new issues, armed with the necessary expert knowledge and free deliberation that takes into account concrete people's needs and demands.

As such, Lenin's politics is the true counterpoint not only to the Third Way pragmatic opportunism, but also to the marginalist Leftist attitude of what Lacan called *le narcissisme de la chose perdue*. What a true Leninist and a political conservative have in common is the fact that they reject what one could call liberal Leftist "irresponsibility" (advocating grand projects of solidarity, freedom, etc., yet ducking out when one has to pay the price for it in the guise of concrete and often "cruel" political measures): like an authentic conservative, a true Leninist is not afraid to *pass to the act*, to assume all the consequences, unpleasant as they may be, of realizing his political project. Rudyard Kipling (whom Brecht admired) despised British liberals who advocated freedom and justice, while silently counting on the Conservatives to do the necessary dirty work for them; the same can be said for the liberal Leftist's (or democratic Socialist's) relationship towards Leninist Communists: liberal Leftists reject the Social Democratic "compromise," they want a true revolution, yet they shirk the actual price to be paid for it and thus prefer to adopt the attitude of a Beautiful Soul and to keep their hands clean. In contrast to this false radical Leftist's position (who wants true democracy for the people, but without the secret police to fight counter-revolution, without their academic privileges being threatened), a Leninist, like a Conservative, is *authentic* in the sense of *fully assuming the consequences of his choice*, i.e. of being fully aware of what it actually means to take power and to exert it.

The return to Lenin is the endeavor to retrieve the unique moment when a thought already transposes itself into a collective organization, but does not yet fix itself into an Institution (the established Church, the IPA, the Stalinist Party-State). It aims neither at nostalgically *reenacting* the "good old revolutionary times," nor at the opportunistic-pragmatic *adjustment* of the old program to "new conditions," but at *repeating*, in the present world-wide conditions, the Leninist gesture of initiating a political project that would undermine the totality of the global liberal–capitalist world order, and, furthermore, a project that would unabashedly assert itself as acting on behalf of truth, as intervening in the present global situation from the standpoint of its repressed truth. What Christianity did with regard to the Roman Empire, this global "multiculturalist" polity, we should do with regard to today's Empire.[2]

One

GNOSTICISM? NO, THANKS!

The gap that separates Gnosticism from Christianity concerns the basic question of "who is responsible for the origin of death":

> If you can accept a God who coexists with death camps, schizophrenia, and AIDS, yet remains all-powerful and somehow benign, then you have faith . . . . If you *know* yourself as having an affinity with the alien, or stranger God, cut off from this world, then you are a Gnostic.[1]

These, then, are the minimal coordinates of Gnosticism: each human being has deep in himself a divine spark which unites him with the Supreme Good; in our daily existence, we are unaware of this spark, since we are kept ignorant by being caught in the inertia of the material reality. How does such a view relate to Christianity proper? Is it that Christ had to sacrifice himself in order to pay for the sins of His Father who created such an imperfect world? Perhaps, this Gnostic Divinity, the evil Creator of our material world, is the clue to the relationship between Judaism and Christianity, the "vanishing mediator" repressed by both of them: the Mosaic figure of the severe God of Commandments is a fake whose mighty apparition is here to conceal the fact that we are dealing with a confused idiot who botched up the job of creation; in a displaced way, Christianity then acknowledges this fact (Christ dies in order to redeem his father in the eyes of humanity).[2]

Along the same lines, the Cathars, the Christian heresy par excellence, posited two opposed divinities: on the one hand, the infinitely good God who, however, is strangely impotent, unable to CREATE anything; on the other, the Creator of our material universe who is none other than the Devil himself (identical to the God of the Old Testament) – the visible, tangible world in its entirety is a diabolical phenomenon, a manifestation of Evil. The Devil is able to create, but is a sterile creator; this sterility is confirmed by the fact that the Devil succeeded in producing a wretched universe in which, despite all his efforts, he never contrived anything lasting. Man is thus a divided creature: as an entity of flesh and blood, he is a creation of the Devil. However, the Devil was not able to create spiritual Life, so he was supposed to have asked the good God for help; in his bounty, God agreed to assist the Devil, this depressingly sterile creator, by breathing a soul into the body of lifeless clay. The Devil succeeded in perverting this spiritual flame by causing the Fall, i.e. by drawing the first couple into the carnal union which consummated their position as the creatures of matter.

Why did the Church react in such a violent way to this Gnostic narrative? Not because of the Cathars' radical Otherness (the dualist belief in the Devil as the counter-agent to the good God; the condemnation of every procreation and fornication, i.e. the disgust at Life in its cycle of generation and corruption), but because these "strange" beliefs which seemed so shocking to the Catholic orthodoxy "were precisely those that had the appearance of stemming logically from orthodox contemporary doctrine. That was why they were considered so dangerous."[3] Was the Catharist dualism not simply a consequent development of the Catholic belief in the Devil? Was the Catharist rejection of fornication also the consequence of the Catholic notion that concupiscence is inherently "dirty," and has merely to be tolerated within the confines of marriage, so that marriage is ultimately a compromise with human weakness? In short, what the Cathars offered was the *inherent transgression* of the official Catholic dogma, its disavowed logical conclusion. And, perhaps, this allows us to propose a more general definition of what heresy is: in order for an ideological edifice to occupy the hegemonic place and legitimize the existing power relations, it HAS to compromise its founding radical message – and the ultimate "heretics" are simply those who reject this compromise, sticking to the original message. (Recall the fate of Saint Francis: by insisting on the vow of poverty of the true Christian, by refusing integration into the existing social edifice, he came very close to being excommunicated – he was embraced by the Church only after the necessary "rearrangements" were made, which flattened this edge that posed a threat to the existing feudal relations.)

Heidegger's notion of *Geworfenheit*, of "being-thrown" into a concrete historical situation, could be of some help here. *Geworfenheit* is to be opposed both to the standard humanism and to the Gnostic tradition. In the humanist vision, a human being belongs to this earth: he should be fully at home on its surface, able to realize his potential through the active, productive exchange with it. As the young Marx put it, earth is man's "anorganic body." Any notion that we do not belong to this earth, that Earth is a fallen universe, a prison for our soul striving to liberate itself from the material inertia, is dismissed as life-denying alienation. For the Gnostic tradition, on the other hand, the human Self is not created, it is a preexisting Soul thrown into a foreign inhospitable environment. The pain of our daily lives is not the result of our sin (of Adam's Fall), but of the fundamental glitch in the structure of the material universe itself which was created by defective demons; consequently, the path of salvation does not reside in overcoming our sins, but in overcoming our *ignorance*, in transcending the world of material appearances by way of achieving the true Knowledge.

What both these positions share is the notion that there is a home, a "natural" place for man: either this world of the "noosphere" from which we fell into this world and for which our souls long, or Earth itself. Heidegger points the way out of this predicament: what if we effectively are "thrown" into this world, never fully at home in it, always dislocated, "out of joint," and what if this dislocation is our constitutive, primordial condition, the very horizon of our being? What if there is no previous "home" out of which we were thrown into this world, what if this very dislocation grounds man's ex-static opening to the world?

As Heidegger emphasizes in *Sein und Zeit*, the fact that there is no *Sein* (being) without *Dasein* (being-there) does NOT mean that, if the *Dasein* were to disappear, no things would remain. Entities would continue to be, but they would not be disclosed within a horizon of meaning – there would have been no *world*. This is why Heidegger speaks of *Dasein* and not of man or subject: subject is OUTSIDE the world and then relates to it, generating the pseudo-problems of the correspondence of our representations to the external world, of the world's existence, etc.; man is an entity INSIDE the world. *Dasein*, in contrast to both of them, is the ex-static relating to the entities within a horizon of meaning, which is in advance "thrown" into the world, in the midst of disclosed entities.

However, there still remains a "naive" question: if entities are there as Real prior to *Lichtung* (clearing), how do the two ultimately relate? *Lichtung* had somehow to "explode" from the closure of mere entities – did not Schelling struggle (and fail) with this ultimate problem in his *Weltalter* drafts, which aimed at deploying the emergence of *logos* out of the proto-cosmic Real of divine drives? Are we to take the risk of endorsing the philosophical potentials of the modern physics whose results seem to point towards a gap/opening discernible already in the pre-ontological nature itself? Furthermore, what if THIS is the danger of technology: that the world itself, its opening, will disappear; that we'll return to the prehuman mute being of entities without *Lichtung*?

It is against this background that one should also approach the relationship between Heidegger and Oriental thought. In his exchange with Heidegger, Medard Boss proposes that, in contrast to Heidegger, in Indian thought, the Clearing (*Lichtung*) in which beings appear does not need man (*Dasein*) as the "shepherd of being" – a human being is merely one of the domains of "standing in the clearing" which shines forth in and for itself. Man unites himself with the Clearing through his self-annihilation, through the ecstatic immersion into the Clearing.[4] This difference is crucial: the fact that man is the unique "shepherd of Being" introduces the notion of the epochal *historicity* of the Clearing itself, a motif totally lacking in Indian thought. Already in the 1930s, Heidegger emphasized the fundamental "derangement (*Ver-Rücktheit*)" that the emergence of Man introduces into the order of entities: the event of Clearing is in itself an *Ent-Eignen*, a radical and thorough distortion, with no possibility of "returning to the undistorted Order". *Ereignis* is co-substantial with the distortion/derangement, it is NOTHING BUT its own distortion. This dimension is, again, totally lacking in Oriental thought – and Heidegger's ambivalence is symptomatic here. On the one hand, he repeatedly insisted that the main task of Western thought today is to defend the Greek breakthrough, the founding gesture of the "West," the overcoming of the pre-philosophical mythical "Asiatic" universe, against the renewed "Asiatic" threat – the greatest opposite of the West is "the mythical in general and the Asiatic in particular."[5] On the other hand, he gave occasional hints as to how his notions of Clearing and Event resonate with the Oriental notion of the primordial Void.

The philosophical overcoming of the myth is not simply a letting-behind of the mythical, but a constant struggle with(in) it: philosophy needs the recourse to myth, not only for external reasons, in order to explain its conceptual teaching to the uneducated masses, but inherently, to "suture" its own conceptual edifice where it fails in reaching its innermost core, from Plato's myth of the cave to Freud's myth of the primordial father and Lacan's myth of *lamella*. Myth is thus the Real of *logos*: the foreign intruder, impossible to get rid of, impossible to remain fully within it. Therein resides the lesson of Adorno's and Horkheimer's *Dialectic of Enlightenment*: enlightenment always already "contaminates" the mythical naive immediacy; enlightenment itself is mythical, i.e. its own grounding gesture *repeats* the mythical operation. And what is "postmodernism" if not the ultimate *defeat* of the Enlightenment in its very triumph: when the dialectic of enlightenment reaches its apogee, the dynamic, rootless postindustrial society *directly generates its own myth*. The technological reductionism of the cognitivist partisans of Artificial

Intelligence and the pagan mythic imaginary of sorcery, of mysterious magic powers, etc., are strictly the two sides of the same phenomenon: the defeat of modernity in its very triumph.

The ultimate postmodern irony is thus the strange exchange between Europe and Asia: at the very moment when, at the level of the "economic infrastructure," "European" technology and capitalism are triumphing world-wide, at the level of "ideological superstructure," the Judeo-Christian legacy is threatened in the European space itself by the onslaught of the New Age "Asiatic" thought, which, in its different guises, from the "Western Buddhism" (today's counterpoint to Western Marxism, as opposed to the "Asiatic" Marxism–Leninism) to different "Taos," is establishing itself as the hegemonic ideology of global capitalism.[6] Therein resides the highest speculative identity of the opposites in today's global civilization: although "Western Buddhism" presents itself as the remedy against the stressful tension of the capitalist dynamics, allowing us to uncouple and retain inner peace and *Gelassenheit*, it actually functions as its perfect ideological supplement. One should mention here the well-known topic of "future shock," i.e. of how, today, people are no longer psychologically able to cope with the dazzling rhythm of technological development and the social changes that accompany it – things simply move too fast. Before one can accustom oneself to an invention, it is already supplanted by a new one, so that more and more one lacks the most elementary "cognitive mapping."

The recourse to Taoism or Buddhism offers a way out of this predicament which definitely works better than the desperate escape into old traditions: instead of trying to cope with the accelerating rhythm of technological progress and social changes, one should rather renounce the very endeavor to retain control over what goes on, rejecting it as the expression of the modern logic of domination – one should, instead, "let oneself go," drift along, while retaining an inner distance and indifference towards the mad dance of this accelerated process, a distance based on the insight that all this social and technological upheaval is ultimately just a non-substantial proliferation of semblances which do not really concern the innermost kernel of our being . . . One is almost tempted to resuscitate here the old infamous Marxist cliché of religion as the "opium of the people," as the imaginary supplement of the terrestrial misery: the "Western Buddhist" meditative stance is arguably the most efficient way, for us, to fully participate in the capitalist dynamic while retaining the appearance of mental sanity. If Max Weber were alive today, he would definitely write a second, supplementary, volume to his *Protestant Ethic*, entitled *The Taoist Ethic and the Spirit of Global Capitalism*.[7]

"Western Buddhism" thus perfectly fits the *fetishist* mode of ideology in our allegedly "post-ideological" era, as opposed to its traditional *symptomal* mode, in which the ideological lie which structures our perception of reality is threatened by symptoms qua "returns of the repressed," cracks in the fabric of the ideological lie. Fetish is effectively a kind of *inverse* of the symptom. That is to say, the symptom is the exception which disturbs the surface of the false appearance, the point at which the repressed Other Scene erupts, while fetish is the embodiment of the Lie which enables us to sustain the unbearable truth. Let us take the case of the death of a beloved person: in the case of a symptom, I "repress" this death, I try not to think about it, but the repressed trauma returns in the symptom; in the case of a fetish, on the contrary, I "rationally" fully accept this death, and yet I cling to the fetish, to some feature that embodies for me the disavowal of this death. In this sense, a fetish can play a very constructive role in allowing us to cope with the harsh reality: fetishists are not dreamers lost in their private worlds, they are thoroughly "realists," able to accept the way things effectively are – since they have their fetish to which they can cling in order to cancel the full impact of reality. In Nevil Shute's World War II melodramatic novel *Requiem For a WREN*, the heroine survives her lover's death without any visible traumas, she goes on with her life and is even able to talk rationally about the lover's death – because she still has the dog who was the lover's favored pet. When, some time after, the dog is accidentally run over by a truck, she collapses and her entire world disintegrates . . . [8] In this precise sense, money is for Marx a fetish: I pretend to be a rational, utilitarian subject, well aware how things truly stand – but I embody my disavowed belief in the money-fetish . . . Sometimes, the line between the two is almost indiscernible: an object can function as the symptom (of a repressed desire) and almost simultaneously as a fetish (embodying the belief which we officially renounce). For instance, a relic of the dead person, a piece of his/her clothing, can function as a fetish (in it, the dead person magically continues to live) and as a symptom (the disturbing detail that brings to mind his/her death). Is this ambiguous tension not homologous to that between the phobic and the fetishist object? The structural role is in both cases the same: if this exceptional element is disturbed, the whole system collapses. Not only does the subject's false universe collapse if he is forced to confront the meaning of his symptom; the opposite also holds, i.e. the subject's "rational" acceptance of the way things are dissolves when his fetish is taken away from him.

So, when we are bombarded by claims that in our post-ideological cynical era nobody believes in the proclaimed ideals, when we encounter a person who claims he is cured of any beliefs, accepting social reality the way it really is, one should always counter such claims with the question: OK, but *where is the fetish which enables you to (pretend to) accept reality "the way it is"?* "Western Buddhism" is such a fetish: it enables you to fully participate in the frantic pace of the capitalist game while sustaining the perception that you are not really in it, that you are well aware how worthless this spectacle is – what really matters to you is the peace of the inner Self to which you know you can always withdraw . . . (In a further specification, one should note that fetish can function in two opposite ways: either its role remains unconscious – as in the case of Shute's heroine who was unaware of the fetish-role of the dog – or you think that the fetish is that which really matters, as in the case of a Western Buddhist unaware that the "truth" of his existence is the social involvment which he tends to dismiss as a mere game.)

FROM THE THING TO OBJECTS A . . . AND BACK

However, linking psychoanalysis and anti-capitalism is discredited today. If one discards the two standard versions, the old topic of the infamous "anal character" as the libidinal foundation of capitalism (the exemplary case of psychological reductionism, if there ever was one), and its inversion, the no less old Freudo–Marxian simplifications (sexual repression is the result of social domination and exploitation, so that classless society will bring about sexual liberation, the full capacity to enjoy life), the reproach that pops up almost automatically against the notion of the inherently anti-capitalist nature of psychoanalysis is that the relationship between these two fields of knowledge is inherently antagonistic: from the standard Marxist point of view, psychoanalysis is unable to comprehend how the libidinal structure it portrays (the Oedipal constellation) is rooted in specific historical circumstances, which is why it elevates contingent historical obstacles into an a priori of the human condition, while for psychoanalysis, Marxism relies on a simplified, psychologically naive, notion of man, which is why it is unable to grasp why attempts at liberation necessarily give rise to new forms of domination.

One is tempted to describe this tension as the one between comedy and tragedy (in the Medieval sense of the terms): Marxism is yet another comedy, another narrative of human history as the process ending in the final redemption, while the view of psychoanalysis is inherently tragic, that of an irresolvable antagonism, of every human act going awry, ruined by unintended "collateral damage." Today's political philosophers like to point out how, *within the domain of mass psychology itself*, psychoanalysis cannot account for the emergence of the collectives which are not "crowds" grounded in primordial crime and guilt or unified under a totalitarian leader, but united in a shared solidarity. What about the magic moments when, all of a sudden, people *are no longer afraid*, when they become aware that, ultimately, to quote the well-known words, they have nothing to fear but the fear itself, that the hypnotizing authority of their masters is the "reflexive determination" (Hegel) of their own submissive attitude towards them?

It was Pascal who pointed out that people do not treat a certain person as a king because he is a king – it is rather that this certain person appears as a king because people treat him as one. Psychoanalysis doesn't seem to allow for such magic ruptures which momentarily break the inexorable chain of tragic necessity: within its scope, every rebellion against authority is ultimately self-defeating; it ends up in the return of the repressed authority in the guise of guilt or self-destructive impulses. On the other hand, psychoanalysts rightly focus on the catastrophic consequences of the radical revolutionary endeavors: the overthrowing of the *ancien regime* brought about even harsher forms of totalitarian domination . . . It's the old story of the revolutionary fools versus the conservative knaves.

So where does all this leave us? The first point to emphasize is that Lacan was well aware of the historical constellation within which psychoanalysis – not as a theory, but as a specific intersubjective practice, a unique form of social link – could have emerged: the capitalist society in which intersubjective relations are mediated by money. Money – paying the analyst – is necessary in order to keep him out of circulation, to avoid getting him involved in the imbroglio of passions which generated the patient's pathology. The psychoanalyst is thus effectively a kind of "prostitute of the mind," having recourse to money for the same reason some prostitutes like to be paid so that they can get sex without personal involvement, maintaining their distance – here, we encounter the function of money at its purest. And the same holds when, today, the Jewish community demands money for their suffering in the Holocaust: they are not indulging in cheap bargaining – it is not that thereby the perpetrators can simply pay the debt and buy their peace. One should recall here Lacan's claim that money's original role is to function as the impossible equivalent for that which has NO PRICE, for desire itself. So, paradoxically, financially recompensing the victims of the Holocaust does not relieve us from our guilt – it rather enables us to acknowledge this guilt as indelible.

Gilles Deleuze's and Félix Guattari's *Anti-Oedipus*[9] was the last great attempt to combine in a subversive synthesis the Marxist and the psychoanalytic traditions. They fully recognized the revolutionary, deterritorializing impact of capitalism, which, in its inexorable dynamics, undermines all stable traditional forms of human interaction; they approached capitalism with the view that its deterritorialization is not thorough enough, that it generates new reterritorializations – a verbatim repetition of the Marxist claim that the ultimate obstacle to capitalism is capitalism itself, i.e. that capitalism unleashes a dynamics it will no longer be able to contain; far from being outdated, this claim seems to gain actuality with today's growing deadlocks of globalization in which the inherently antagonistic nature of capitalism belies its world-wide triumph. However, the problem is: is it still possible to imagine Communism (or another form of post-capitalist society) as a formation which sets free the deterritorializing dynamics of capitalism, liberating it of its inherent constraints? Marx's fundamental vision was that a new, higher social order (Communism) is possible, an order that would not only maintain, but even raise to a higher degree and effectively fully release the potential of the self-increasing spiral of productivity which, in capitalism, on account of its inherent obstacle/contradiction, is again and again thwarted by socially destructive economic crises.

What Marx overlooked is that, to put it in the standard Derridean terms, this inherent obstacle/antagonism as the "condition of impossibility" of the full deployment of the productive forces is simultaneously its "condition of possibility": if we abolish the obstacle, the inherent contradiction of capitalism, we do not get the fully unleashed drive to productivity finally delivered of its impediment, but we lose precisely this productivity that seemed to be generated and simultaneously thwarted by capitalism – if we take away the obstacle, the very potential thwarted by this obstacle dissipates . . . Therein would reside a possible Lacanian critique of Marx, focusing on the ambiguous overlapping between surplus-value and surplus-enjoyment. So the critics of Communism were in a way right when they claimed that Marxian Communism is an impossible fantasy – what they did not perceive is that Marxian Communism, this notion of a society of pure unleashed productivity *outside* the frame of capital, was a fantasy inherent to capitalism itself, the capitalist inherent transgression at its purest, a strictly ideological fantasy of maintaining the thrust to productivity generated by capitalism, while getting rid of the "obstacles" and antagonisms that were – as the sad experience of the "really existing capitalism" demonstrates – *the only possible framework of the effective material existence of a society of permanent self-enhancing productivity.*[10]

One should therefore focus on the Lacanian notion of *plus-de-jouir*, where Lacan's proximity and distance towards Marx are at its most extreme. Jacques-Alain Miller discerned in Lacan the movement from the Thing to surplus-enjoyment, vaguely correlative to the passage from the big Other to the small other. When, in *Seminar VII: On the Ethics of Psychoanalysis* (1959–1960),[11] *jouissance* is first fully asserted as the impossible/real foreign kernel, irreducible to the symbolic order, it appears as the horrifying abyss of the Thing which can only be approached in a suicidal heroic act of transgression, of excluding oneself from the symbolic community – the Thing is the stuff tragic heroes like Oedipus or Antigone are made of, its lethal blinding intensity forever marks those who enter its event horizon. Its best figures are ghastly spectres like de Maupassant's *horla*, E.A. Poe's abyss of the maelstrom, up to the Alien in Ridley Scott's film of the same name, and the frozen Medusa's gaze is the ultimate image of the subject encountering the Thing. What, on the contrary, we find in *Seminar XX (Encore)*[12] is the dispersed multitude of *jouissances*, the proliferation of *sinthoms* (Lacan's neologism: the symptom which synthetizes – holds together – the subject's Universe; there is an echo here of Saint Thomas and the saint, ÎLE SAINT HOMME), particular and contingent "tics" which give body to *jouissance*, best exemplified by the innumerable gadgets with which technology is bombarding us daily.

The reference to capitalism is here deliberate and crucial: the late capitalism, the so-called "society of consumption," is no longer the Order sustained by some founding Prohibition which calls to be transgressed in a heroic act – in the generalized perversion of late capitalism, transgression itself is solicited, we are daily bombarded by gadgets and social forms which not only enable us to live with our perversions, but even directly conjure new perversions. Recall, in the sexual domain proper, all the gadgets invented to bring diversity and new excitement into our sexual lives, from lotions that should enhance our potency and pleasure to different outfits and instruments (rings, provocative dresses, whips and chains, vibrators and other artificial prosthetic organs, not to mention pornography and other direct stimulators of the mind): they do not simply incite the "natural" sexual desire, they rather *supplement* it in the Derridean sense, giving it an irreducible "perverse," excessive and derailed, twist. They – all this (often boring and repetitive) proliferation of gadgets – render most directly what Lacan called *objets petit a*. Among America's best-selling toys in the Summer of 2000 was Death Row Marv

(McFarlane Toys, $24.99), in which a man strapped into an electric chair bombards his executioner with rough and obscene remarks (i.e. you, the customer), almost begging you to light him up with jolts of electricity by pushing the appropriate button. And what about the Electric Chair Game arcades at various parks, not only in the US, but also in Europe, where you are strapped in to receive the controlled dose of electricity (voluntarily administered): "winning" involves staying in the chair until the machine declares you dead, while losers release the electrodes early. Even the ultimate act of the exercise of state power can be turned into a gadget that provides obscene pleasure . . . Therein resides the libidinal economy of the capitalist "consumption": in the production of objects which do not simply meet or satisfy an already given need, but create the need they claim to satisfy (the publicity usually operates in such a way that the consumer "becomes aware of desires they were not even aware they possessed"), giving the ultimate twist to Marx's old claim that production creates the need for consumption, for the objects it produces. Which is why these objects are no longer (as in Lacan of the 1950s, the 1960s) constrained to the "natural" series of oral object, anal object, voice, gaze, and phallus, but comprise the proliferating multitude of cultural sublimation, which, however, is strictly correlative to a certain lack – the excess of capitalist consumption always functions as the reaction to a fundamental lack:

> The notion of *plus-de-jouir* serves to expand the register of
> the *objets a* beyond those that can be termed as natural, into
> the sphere of industry, culture, sublimation, everything
> potentially able to fill the Phi, without exhausting it, of course.
> These trivial *objets a* abound in society, inducing desire and

occluding, if only for an instant, the *manque-à-jouir* . . . .
Jouir, certainly, but only in small quantities. Lacan calls
them *lichettes*, little bits of *jouissance*. Modern society
is full of substitutes of *jouissance*, in fact petty trifles. The
little bits of *jouissance* set the tone for a lifestyle and for a
mode-de-jouir."[13]

Crucial is here the *asymmetrical* relationship of lack and excess: the proliferation of *objets a* generates the surplus-enjoyment which fills in the lack of *jouissance*, and although these *objets a* never provide "the thing itself," although they are semblances which always fall short of the full *jouissance*, they are nonetheless experienced as excessive, as the *surplus*-enjoyment – in short, in them, the "not enough," the falling short, *coincides with the excess*. Speculative as these propositions may sound, do they not render our daily experience when we have recourse to the innumerable sexual gadgets: they are in excess, they endeavor to give an additional "perverse" twist to our sexual activity, yet, simultaneously, they are pale shadows that somehow lack the substantial density of the Real Thing. The paradox to be endorsed here is that there is no "zero level" substantial *jouissance*, with regard to which *objets a* render the proliferation of excesses: *jouissance* "as such" is an excess, its paradox is the same as that of the electron in elementary particle physics (the mass of each element in our reality is composed of its mass at rest plus the surplus provided by the acceleration of its movement; however, an electron's mass at rest is zero, its mass consists only of the surplus generated by the acceleration of its movement, as if we are dealing with a nothing which acquires some deceptive substance only by magically spinning itself into an excess of itself).

Lacan targets this lack of *jouissance* when he insist that "there is no such thing as the sexual rapport" – there are, of course, sexual relations, the multiple improvised forms in which individuals interact in order to obtain sexual pleasure; however, we have to invent these forms precisely in order to supplement the lack of the "natural" rapport itself. As Miller emphasizes, *Seminar XX*:

> is indeed the seminar of non-rapports. All the terms that insured some sort of conjunction – the Other, the Name-of-the-Father, the phallus – and were deemed primordial, even transcendental, since they conditioned all experience, are now diminished to the status of mere connectors. In lieu of the transcendental terms of structure, which belong to an autonomous dimension anterior to and conditioning experience, there is the supremacy of praxis. In lieu of the transcendental structure, there is a sort of social pragmatism.[14]

In short: in lieu of the proto-transcendental structural a priori of the symbolic Order, we get the improvised multitude of the ways human beings, fundamentally solitary, each of them ultimately constrained to the masturbatory *jouissance* of his/her own body ("There is no such thing as a sexual rapport" implies that *jouissance* is essentially idiotic and solitary),[15] try to improvise and assemble some semblance of relating to and interacting with their others. How far are we here from the "structuralist" Lacan's notion of the big Other as the symbolic order which in advance predetermines the subject's acts, so that we even do not speak, but "are spoken" by the Other! How far are we from "desire as the desire of the Other," from the notion of the Unconscious as the "discourse of the Other"! Lacan's individualism is not naturalist: his idea is not that humans are lone self-immersed individuals "by nature," but that the passage from animal copulation to properly human sexuality affects the human animal in such a way that it causes the human animal's radical self-withdrawal, so that the zero-level of human sexuality is not the "straight" sexual intercourse, but the solitary act of masturbation sustained by fantasizing[16] – the passage from this self-immersion to involvement with an Other, to finding pleasure in the Other's body, is by no means "natural," it involves a series of traumatic cuts, leaps and inventive improvisations. Sexual contact with the Other is not a matter of the symbolic Law, but of perverse contracts, of fragile negotiated figurations which can always fall apart. The Name-of-the-Father is no longer the ultimate guarantee of sexuality (as Lacan still claimed in the very last page of the *Four Fundamental Concepts*, where we can read that a bearable sexual relation can take place only under the protective shield of the Name-of-the-Father),[17] but simply one in the series of perverse contracts, of temporary inventions which, for contingent historical reasons, were taken up and held longer than others – therein resides the meaning of Lacan's pun in writing *perversion* as *pere-version*: the father's version (the paternal Law) is just one in the series of perversions:

What concerns Lacan in *Seminar XX* is the disclosure of everything that in *jouissance* is *jouissance* One, that is, *jouissance* without the Other. The very title of the seminar, *Encore*, should be homophonically inferred as *en-corps*, in-the-body. Here, the body occupies the center of the stage . . . it implies the rediscovery, in psychoanalysis, of what succeeds today in the social link, modern individualism, and the ambiguity that results in everything that is rapport and community. The conjugal bond, for instance, where even those who are deemed conservative, who revere routine as

> well as tradition, yield to the invention of new forms of rapport
> sponsored by political consensus. *Jouissance* envisages as a
> starting point constitutes the true foundation of what ensues
> as extension, even insanity, in contemporary individualism.[18]

The paradox here is, again, the overlapping of opposites. In his *Consciousness Explained*, Daniel Dennett, the great proponent of cognitivist evolutionism, (ironically, no doubt, but nonetheless with an underlying serious intent) acknowledges the closeness of his "Pandemonium" theory of human mind to Cultural Studies deconstructionism:

> Imagine my mixed emotions when I discovered that before I
> could get my version of the idea of [the Self as the Center of
> Narrative Gravity] properly published in a book, it had already
> been satirized in a novel, David Lodge's *Small World*. It is
> apparently a hot theme among the deconstructionists.[19]

Furthermore, a whole school of cyberspace theorists advocate the notion that cyberspace phenomena render palpable in our everyday experience the deconstructionist "decentered subject": one should endorse the "dissemination" of the unique Self into a multiplicity of competing agents, into a "collective mind", a plurality of self-images without a global coordinating center, which is operative in cyberspace, and disconnect it from pathological trauma – playing in virtual spaces enables me to discover new aspects of "me", a wealth of shifting identities, of masks without a "real" person behind, and thus to experience the ideological mechanism of the production of Self, the immanent violence and arbitrariness of this production/construction . . .

So, at the same time that cognitivists and deconstructionists, these two official enemies, share the claim that there is no "substantial" Self which would precede the open field of contingent social interaction, and when even the Western Buddhists join in this chorus with the insight that my Self is nothing but the groundless bundle of elusive and heterogeneous (mental) events, our experience is more and more that of an isolated Self immersed in its hallucinatory sphere. Therein resided already the lesson of the postmodern deconstruction of the Self: depriving the Self of any substantial content ends in radical subjectivization, in the loss of the firm objective reality itself (according to the postmodern mantra, there is no firm reality, just the multitude of contingent social constructions).

No wonder that Leibniz is one of the predominant philosophical references of the cyberspace theorists: what reverberates today is not only his dream of a universal computing machine, but the uncanny resemblance between his ontological vision of monadology and today's emerging cyberspace community in which global harmony and solipsism strangely coexist. That is to say, does our immersion into cyberspace not go hand in hand with our reduction to a Leibnizean monad which, although "without windows" that would directly open up to external reality, mirrors in itself the entire universe? Are we not more and more monads with no direct windows onto reality, interacting alone with the PC screen, encountering only the virtual simulacra, and yet immersed more than ever in the global network, synchronously communicating with the entire globe? The impasse which Leibniz tried to solve by way of introducing the notion of the "preestablished harmony" between the monads, guaranteed by God Himself, the supreme, all-encompassing monad, repeats itself today, in the guise of the problem of communication: how does each of us know that he or she is in touch with the "real other" behind the screen, not only with spectral simulacra?[20]

Two theoretical connections impose themselves here: Richard Rorty (mentioned by Miller himself), and the theory of "reflexive society" elaborated by Ulrich Beck.[21] From the standpoint of Lacan's last paradigm, it could be argued Rorty emerges as THE philosopher of our epoch, with his neo-Pragmatist notion that language is not a transcendental a priori of our society, and that it cannot be grounded in the Habermasian way in a set of universal norms, since it is a *bricolage* of patched-up procedures? And does not Lacan's emphasis on the improvised and negotiated character of all social links point towards the notion of "reflexive society" in which all patterns of interaction, from the forms of sexual partnership up to ethnic identity itself, have to be renegotiated/reinvented?

The case of Muslims as an ethnic, not merely religious, group in Bosnia is exemplary here: during the entire history of Yugoslavia, Bosnia was the place of potential tension and dispute, the locale in which the struggle between Serbs and Croats for the dominant role was fought. The problem was that the largest group in Bosnia was neither the Orthodox Serbs nor the Catholic Croats, but Muslims whose ethnic origins were always disputed – are they Serbs or Croats? (This role of Bosnia even left its trace in idiom: in all ex-Yugoslav nations, the expression "So Bosnia is quiet!" was used to signal that any threat of a conflict was successfully defused.) In order to forestall this focus of potential (and actual) conflicts, in the 1960s the ruling Communists imposed a miraculously simple invention: they proclaimed Muslims an autochthonous ETHNIC community, not just a religious group, so that Muslims were able to avoid pressure to identify themselves either as Serbs or as Croats. What was in the beginning a pragmatic political artifice gradually caught on: Muslims effectively started to perceive themselves as a nation, systematically manufacturing their tradition, etc. However, even today, there remains an element of a reflected *choice* in their identity: during the post-Yugoslav war in Bosnia, one was ultimately forced to CHOOSE his/her ethnic identity – when a militia stopped a person, asking him/her threateningly "Are you a Serb or a Muslim?", the question did not refer to the inherited ethnic belonging, i.e. there was always in it an echo of "Which side did you *choose*?" (for example the movie director Emir Kusturica, coming from an ethnically mixed Muslim-Serb family, has chosen the Serb identity). The properly FRUSTRATING dimension of this choice is perhaps best rendered by the situation of having to choose a product in on-line shopping, where one has to make the almost endless series of choices: if you want it with X, press A, if not, press B . . . The paradox is that what is thoroughly excluded in these post-traditional "reflexive societies," in which we are all the time bombarded with the urge to choose, in which even such "natural" features as sexual orientation and ethnic identification are experienced as a matter of choice, is the basic, authentic, *choice itself*.

Of course, one should avoid here a precipitous full identification: both Rorty and the theory of "reflexive society" lack the Lacanian notion of how the proliferation of improvised and negotiated relations takes place against the background – not simply of the disintegration of old traditional patterns, but of the excess of *jouissance*, how it is a way to cope with this excess, to "gentrify" it. On the other hand, with regard to Lacan, this relating of the "paradigms of *jouissance*" to concrete socio-historical formations compels us to reconceptualize

Lacan's theory itself: when Miller endeavors to discern the succession of the different "paradigms of *jouissance*" in Lacan's teaching, one is, in a first move, tempted to *historicize* this succession, i.e. to see in it not only the inherent logic of Lacan's development, but the reflection of the fundamental shifts in post-World War II French society; a different Lacan thus appears, the one extremely sensitive to the shifts in the hegemonic ideological trends. Let us constrain ourselves to the key four of the six paradigms identified by Miller:

(1) First, we have the "structuralist" Lacan with the emphasis on the quasi-transcendental determining role of the "big Other," of the symbolic order which sets in advance the possible coordinates of human life. *Jouissance* is here conceived of as the false imaginary fullness which bears witness of how the subject avoided the truth of his/her desire: the task of psychoanalysis is to dissolve the symptoms (in which the subject enjoys) through the process of interpretation – what should replace *jouissance* is the full assumption of the *meaning* of the symptom. It is more than an irrelevant accident that this paradigm is accompanied by Lacan's viciously anti-American rhetoric: this, to put it bluntly, is the conservative Gaullist Lacan, deploring the decay of authentic symbolic authority.

(2) Then, in the next paradigm, *Jouissance* as the impossible Real which eludes the big Other reasserts itself with a vengeance as the terrifying abyss of the Thing – the adoration of the Structure and its Law reverts to the fascination with the heroic suicidal transgressive gesture which excludes the subject from the symbolic community. As to its socio-political background, one should bear in mind that, when Lacan was writing his famous interpretation

of *Antigone*, he was bringing the transcriptions of his lectures to his daughter Laurence Bataille, who was imprisoned because of her engagement in the Algerian struggle for independence. Is this not Lacan's reaction to the first cracks which appeared in the solid edifice of post-World War II French society?

(3) *Seminar XVII* (1969–1970) on the four discourses[22] is Lacan's response to the events of 1968 – its premise is best captured as his reversal of the well-known anti-structuralist graffito "Structures do not walk on the streets!" – if anything, this Seminar endeavors to demonstrate how structures DO walk on the streets, i.e. how structural shifts CAN account for social outbursts like that of 1968. Instead of the one Symbolic Order with its set of a priori rules which guarantee social cohesion, we get the matrix of the passages from one to another discourse: Lacan's interest is focused on the passage from the discourse of the Master to the discourse of University as the hegemonic discourse in contemporary society. No wonder that the revolt was located in the universities: as such, it merely signalled the shift to the new forms of domination in which the scientific discourse serves to legitimize the relations of domination. Lacan's underlying premise is thus again skeptically conservative – Lacan's diagnosis is best captured by his famous retort to the student revolutionaries: "As hysterics, you demand a new master. You will get it!"

(4) Finally, *Seminar XX* provides the libidinal economy of today's postmodern, post-revolutionary, "society of consumption," which began in the US, also became popular in France – the society of "non-rapport" in which all stable forms of social cohesion disintegrate, in which

the idiotic *jouissance* of individuals is socialized only in the mode of fragile and shifting pragmatic inventions and new negotiated customs (the proliferation of new improvised modes of sexual cohabitation instead of the basic matrix of marriage, etc.).

The logic of this succession is thus clear enough: we start with the stable symbolic Order; we proceed to the heroic suicidal attempts to break out of it; when the Order itself seems threatened, we provide the matrix of permutations which accounts for how the revolt itself is just the operator of the passage from one to another form of the social link; finally, we confront the society in which the revolt itself is rendered meaningless, since, in it, transgression itself is not only recuperated, but directly solicited by the system as the very form of its reproduction. To put it in Hegel's terms, the "truth" of the student's transgressive revolt against the Establishment is the emergence of a new establishment in which transgression is part of the game, solicited by the gadgets which organize our life as the permanent dealing with excesses.

Is, then, Lacan's ultimate result a conservative resignation, a kind of closure, or does this approach allow for a radical social change? The first thing to take note of is that the preceding paradigms do not simply disappear in those which follow – they persist, casting a shadow on them. The late capitalist global market society is by no means characterized by the undisputed rule of the proliferating *objets a*: this very society is simultaneously haunted by the prospect of confronting the Thing in its different guises – no longer predominantly the nuclear catastrophe, but the multitude of other catastrophes that loom on the horizon (the ecological catastrophe, the prospect of an asteroid hitting the Earth, up to the microlevel of some virus going crazy and destroying human life). Furthermore, as Miller himself deployed apropos of the notion of extimacy, and as Lacan himself predicted in the early 1970s, does not capitalist globalization give rise to the new racism focusing on the "theft of enjoyment," on the figure of the Other who either threatens to snatch from us the treasure of our "way of life," and/or itself possesses and displays an excessive *jouissance* that eludes our grasp? In short, the passage from the traumatic Thing to *lichettes*, to the "little bits of *jouissance* [which] set the tone for a lifestyle," never fully succeeds, the Thing continues to cast its shadow, so that what we have today is the proliferation of the lifestyle *lichettes* against the background of the ominous Thing, the catastrophe which threatens to destroy the precious balance of our various lifestyles.

This weakness of Miller's description of the paradigms of jouissance has a deeper ground. Today, in a time of continuous rapid changes, from the "digital revolution" to the retreat of old social forms, thought is more than ever exposed to the temptation of "losing its nerve," of precociously abandoning the old conceptual coordinates. The media constantly bombard us with the need to abandon the "old paradigms": if we are to survive, we have to change our most fundamental notions of what constitutes personal identity, society, environment, etc. New Age wisdom claims that we are entering a new "post-human" era; postmodern political thought tells us that we are entering post-industrial societies, in which the old categories of labor, collectivity, class, etc., are theoretical zombies, no longer applicable to the dynamics of modernization. The Third Way ideology and political practice is effectively THE model of this defeat, of this inability to recognize how the New is here to enable the Old to survive.

Against this temptation, one should rather follow the unsurpassed model of Pascal and ask the difficult question: how are we to remain faithful to the Old in the new conditions? ONLY in this way can we generate something effectively New. And the same holds for psychoanalysis: starting with the rise of ego-psychology in the 1930s, psychoanalysts are "losing their nerve," laying down their (theoretical) arms, hastening to concede that the Oedipal matrix of socialization is no longer operative, that we live in times of universalized perversion, that the concept of "repression" is of no use in our permissive times. Unfortunately, even such an astute theoretician as Miller seems to succumb to this temptation, desperately trying to catch up with the alleged post-patriarchal "new times," driven by the fear of losing contact with the latest social developments, and thus proposing dubious fast generalizations, claiming that the symbolic order proper is no longer operative in our society of imaginary semblances, that feminization is acquiring global dimensions, that the very notion of interpretation is rendered inoperative . . . Miller's description of Lacan's last paradigm of *jouissance* exemplifies this failure of conceptual thought, whose lack is filled in by hasty pre-theoretical generalizations.

NO SEX, PLEASE, WE'RE DIGITAL!

Within these coordinates, the cyberspace ideologist's notion of the Self liberating itself from the attachment to its natural body, i.e. turning itself into a virtual entity floating from one to another contingent and temporary embodiment, can present itself as the final scientific-technological realization of the Gnostic dream of the Self getting rid of the decay and inertia of material reality. That is to say, is the notion of the "aetheric" body we can recreate for ourselves in Virtual

Reality not the old Gnostic dream of the immaterial "astral body" come true? So what are we to make of this seemingly convincing argument that cyberspace functions in a Gnostic way, promising to elevate us to a level in which we will be delivered of our bodily inertia, provided with another ethereal body? There are four predominant theoretical attitudes with regard to cyberspace:

(1) The purely technological celebration of the new potentials of supercomputers, nanotechnology and genetic technology;[23]

(2) Its New Age counterpoint, i.e. the emphasis on the Gnostic background that sustains even the most "neutral" scientific research;[24]

(3) The historicist–sociocritical "deconstructionist" deployment of the liberating potentials of cyberspace which, through its blurring of the limits of the Cartesian ego, its identity, monopoly on thought, and attachment to the biological body, allows us to pass from the male–Cartesian–liberal–identitarian subject to the dispersed–cyborgian "posthuman" forms of subjectivity, from the biological body to shifting embodiments;[25]

(4) The Heideggerian philosophical reflections on the implications of digitalization, focusing on the notion of *Dasein* as Being-in-the-World, as the engaged agent thrown into a determinate life-world situation.[26] In this view, the advent of genome and of the technological perspective of the "uploading" of the human mind onto a computer provides the clearest vision of what Heidegger had in mind when he spoke of the "danger" of planetary technology: what is threatened here is the very ex-static essence of *Dasein*, of man as capable of transcending self

by relating to entities within the Clearing of his/her world (significantly, for Heidegger, the very view of the Earth from space signalled the termination of the human essence as dwelling between Heaven and Earth – once we view Earth from space, the Earth is in a way no longer Earth). However, this very "danger" enables us to confront radically the fate of humanity and, perhaps, to outline a different modality of our engagement with technology, the one which, precisely, undermines the Cartesian subject of technological domination.

The first two attitudes share the premise of total disembodiment, of the reduction of the (post)human mind to software pattern freely floating between different embodiments, while the other two assert the finitude of the embodied agent as the ultimate horizon of our existence – to quote Katherine Hayles's concise formulation:

> If my nightmare is a culture inhabited by posthumans who regard their bodies as fashion accessories rather than the ground of being, my dream is a version of the posthuman that embraces the possibilities of information technologies without being seduced by fantasies of unlimited power and disembodied immortality, that recognizes and celebrates finitude as a condition of human being, and that understands human life as embedded in a material world of great complexity, one on which we depend for our continued survival.[27]

One is nonetheless tempted to ask if this solution is not too facile: the moment one takes the fateful step from the immediate (finite, biological) *body* that we "are" to the biotechnological *embodiment* with its shifting and unstable character, one can no longer get rid of the spectre of the "undead" eternal body. Konrad Lorenz made the ambiguous remark that we ourselves (the "actually existing" humanity) are the sought-after "missing link" between animal and man – how are we to read it? Of course, the first association that imposes itself here is the notion that the "actually existing" humanity still dwells in what Marx designated as "pre-history," and that the true human history will begin with the advent of the Communist society; or, in Nietzsche's terms, that man is just a bridge, a passage between animal and over-man. (Not to mention the New Age version: we are entering a new era in which humanity will transform itself into a Global Mind, leaving behind petty individualism.) What Lorenz "meant" was undoubtedly situated along these lines, although with a more humanistic twist: humanity is still immature and barbarian, it had not yet reached the full wisdom. However, an opposite reading also imposes itself: this intermediate status of man IS his greatness, since the human being IS in its very essence a "passage," the finite openness into an abyss.

It is precisely historical traumas like the Holocaust which seem to posit a limit to such a Nietzschean vision. For Nietzsche, if we do not radicalize the Will to Power into the Eternal Recurrence of the Same, the assertion of our Will remains incomplete, we forever remain constrained by the inertia of the past which we did not choose or will, and which, as such, limits the scope of our free self-assertion: only the Eternal Recurrence of the Same changes every "it was" into "it will be," apropos of which I can then say "I willed it thus."

There is an inherent link between the notions of trauma and repetition, signalled in Freud's well-known motto that what one is not able to remember, one is condemned to repeat: a trauma is by definition something one is not able to remember, i.e. to recollect by way of making it part of one's symbolic narrative; as such, it repeats itself indefinitely, returning to haunt the subject – more precisely, what repeats itself is the very failure, impossibility even, to repeat/recollect the trauma properly. Nietzsche's Eternal Recurrence of the Same, of course, aims precisely at such a full recollection: the Eternal Recurrence of the Same ultimately means that there is no longer any traumatic kernel resisting its recollection, that the subject can fully assume his/her past, projecting it into the future as willing its recurrence. Is it, however, effectively possible to assume a subjective stance of actively WILLING the traumatic event to repeat itself indefinitely?

It is here that we confront the Holocaust as an ethical problem: is it possible to sustain the Eternal Recurrence even apropos of the Holocaust, i.e. to adopt also towards it the stance of "I willed it thus"? It is significant how, apropos of the Holocaust, Primo Levi reproduces the old paradox of prohibiting the impossible: "Perhaps one cannot, what is more one must not, understand what happened"[28] – here is an inversion of Kant's "You can, because you must!", namely "You cannot, because you must not!", which abounds in today's religious resistance to genetic manipulations: "One cannot reduce the human spirit to the genes, which is why one should not do it!" What, however, nonetheless distinguishes Levi from the fashionable elevation of the Holocaust into an untouchable transcendent evil is that, at this very point, he introduces the distinction (on which Lacan relies all the time) between understanding and knowledge – he pursues: "We cannot understand it, but we can and must understand from where it springs . . . . If understanding is impossible, knowing is imperative, because what happened could happen again."[29] This knowledge (whose function is precisely to prevent the Recurrence of the Same) is NOT to be opposed to understanding along the lines of ("inner") Understanding versus ("external") Explaining: there is nothing to understand, because the perpetrators themselves did not understand THEMSELVES, they were not "at the height of their acts," i.e. they did not subjectively assume their acts and their consequences. For this reason, one should turn around the standard notion of Holocaust as the historical actualization of "radical (or, rather, diabolical) Evil": Auschwitz is the ultimate argument AGAINST the romanticized notion of "diabolical Evil," of the evil hero who elevates Evil into an a priori principle. As Hannah Arendt was right to emphasize,[30] the unbearable horror of Auschwitz resides in the fact that its perpetrators were NOT Byronesque figures who asserted, like Milton's Satan, "Let Evil be my Good!" – the true cause for alarm resides in the unbridgeable GAP between the horror of what went on and the "human, all too human" character of its perpetrators. Levi himself insisted on the traumatic externality of anti-Semitism (in terms which, in a cruel bit of irony, almost recall the Nazi perception of Jews as external intruders into our social edifice, as a poisonous foreign body):

> There is no rationality in the Nazi hatred: it is a hate that is not in us; it is outside man, it is a poison fruit sprung from the deadly trunk of Fascism, but it is outside and beyond Fascism itself.[31]

When, in his infamous statement, Heidegger puts the annihilation of Jews in the same series with the mechanization of agriculture, as just another example of the total productive mobilization of the modern technology which reduces everything, inclusive of human beings, to the material disponible to the ruthless technological exploitation ("Agriculture is now a motorized food-industry – in essence the same as the manufacturing of corpses in gas chambers and extermination camps, the same as the starving of nations, the same as the manufacture of hydrogen bombs."[32]) this insertion into the series fits Stalinist Socialism, which was a society of total ruthless mobilization, not Nazism, which introduced the excess of anti-Semitic violence. Or, as Primo Levi put it succinctly: "it is possible, even easy, to picture a Socialism without prison camps. A Nazism without concentration camps is, instead, unimaginable."[33]

Even if we concede that the Stalinist terror was the necessary outcome of the Socialist project, we are still dealing with the tragic dimension of an emancipatory project going awry, of an undertaking which fatally misperceived the consequences of its own intervention, in contrast to Nazism which was an anti-emancipatory undertaking going all too well. In other words, the Communist project was one of common brotherhood and welfare, while the Nazi project was one of domination. So when Heidegger alluded to the "inner greatness" of Nazism betrayed by the Nazi ideological peddlers, he again attributed to Nazism something that effectively holds only for Communism: Communism has an "inner greatness," an explosive liberatory potential, while Nazism was perverted through and through, in its very notion: it is simply ridiculous to conceive of the Holocaust as a kind of tragic perversion of the noble Nazi project – its project WAS the Holocaust.[34]

These paradoxes provide the proper background for Michel Houellebecq's *Les particules élémentaires*,[35] the story of radical DESUBLIMATION if there ever was one: in our postmodern "disenchanted" permissive world, sexuality is reduced to an apathetic participation in collective orgies. *Les particules*, a superb example of what some critics perspicuously baptized "Left conservatism," tells the story of two half-brothers: Bruno, a high-school teacher, is an undersexed hedonist, while Michel is a brilliant but emotionally desiccated bio-chemist. Abandoned by their hippie mother when they were small, neither has ever properly recovered; all their attempts at the pursuit of happiness, whether through marriage, the study of philosophy, or the consumption of pornography, merely lead to loneliness and frustration. Bruno ends up in a psychiatric asylum after confronting the meaninglessness of permissive sexuality (the utterly depressing descriptions of the sexual orgies between forty-somethings are among the most excruciating in contemporary literature), while Michel invents a solution: a new self-replicating gene for the post-human desexualized entity. The novel ends with a prophetic vision: in 2040, humanity is replaced by these humanoids who experience no passions proper, no intense self-assertion that can lead to destructive rage.

Almost four decades ago, Michel Foucault dismissed "man" as a figure in the sand that is now being washed away, introducing the (then) fashionable topic of the "death of man." Although Houellebecq stages this disappearance in much more naive literal terms, as the replacement of human-ity with a new post-human species, there is a common denominator between the two: *the disappearance of sexual difference.* In his last works, Foucault envisioned the space of pleasures liberated from sex, and one is tempted to claim that Houelle-becq's post-human society of clones is the realization of the Foucauldian dream of the Selves who practice the "use of pleasures."

While this solution is fantasy at its purest, the deadlock to which it reacts is a real one – how are we to get out of it? The standard way would be to try somehow to resurrect the transgressive erotic passion, following the well-known principle, first fully asserted in the tradition of courtly love, that the only true love is the transgressive prohibited one – we need new Prohibitions, so that a new Tristan and Isolde or Romeo and Juliet will appear . . . The problem is that, in today's permissive society, transgression itself IS the norm. Which, then, is the way out? One should recall here the ultimate lesson of Lacan concerning sublimation: in a way, true sublimation is *exactly the same* as desublimation. Let's take a love relationship: "sublime" is not the cold elevated figure of the Lady who had to remain beyond our reach – if she were to step down from her pedestal, she would turn into a repulsive hag. "Sublime" is the magic *combination* of the two dimensions, when the sublime dimension transpires through the utmost common details of everyday shared life – the "sublime" moment of the love life occurs when the magic dimension transpires even in common everyday acts like washing the dishes or cleaning the apartment. (In this precise sense, sublimation is to be opposed to idealization.)

Perhaps the best way to specify this role of sexual love is through the notion of reflexivity as "the movement whereby that which has been used to generate a system is made, through a changed perspective, to become part of the system it generates."[36] This reflexive appearance of the generating movement within the generated system, in the guise of what Hegel called the "oppositional determination," as a rule takes the form of the opposite: within the material sphere, Spirit appears in the guise of the most inert moment (crane, formless black stone); in the later stage of a revolutionary process when Revolution starts to devour its own children, the political agent which effectively set in motion the process is renegaded into the role of its main obstacle, of the waverers or outright traitors who are not ready to follow the revolutionary logic to its conclusion. Along the same lines, is it not true that, once the socio-symbolic order is fully established, the very dimension which introduced the "transcendent" attitude that defines a human being, namely SEXUALITY, the uniquely human "undead" sexual passion, appears as its very opposite, as the main OBSTACLE to the elevation of a human being to pure spirituality, as that which ties him/her down to the inertia of bodily existence? For this reason, the end of sexuality in the much celebrated "posthuman" self-cloning entity expected to emerge soon, far from opening up the way to pure spirituality, will simultaneously signal the end of what is traditionally designated as the uniquely human spiritual transcendence. All the celebrating of the new "enhanced" possibilities of sexual life that virtual reality offers cannot conceal the fact that, once cloning supplements sexual difference, the game is over.[37]

We all know of Alan Turing's famous "imitation game" which should serve as the test of whether or not a machine can think: we communicate with two computer interfaces, asking them any imaginable question; behind one of the interfaces, there is a human person typing the answers, while behind the other lies a machine. If, based on the answers we get, we cannot tell the intelligent machine from the intelligent human, then, according to Turing, our failure proves that machines can think. What is less well-known is that, in its first formulation, the issue was not to distinguish human from the machine, but man from woman. Why this strange displacement from sexual difference to the difference between human and machine? Was this due to Turing's simple eccentricity (recall his well-known troubles because of his homosexuality)? According to some interpreters, the point is to oppose the two experiments: a successful imitation of a woman's responses by a man (or vice versa) *would not prove anything*, because the gender identity does not depend on the sequences of symbols, while a successful imitation of humanity by a machine would prove that this machine thinks, because "thinking" ultimately is the proper way of sequencing symbols . . . What if, however, the solution to this enigma is much more simple and radical? What if sexual difference is not simply a biological fact, but the Real of an antagonism that *defines humanity*, so that once sexual difference is abolished, a human being effectively becomes indistinguishable from a machine?

One should also emphasize Turing's blindness to the distinction between doing and saying: as many an interpreter has noticed, Turing simply had no sense for the properly SYMBOLIC domain of communication in sexuality, power politics, etc., in which language is used as a rhetorical device, with its referential meaning clearly subordinated to its performative dimension (of seduction, coercion, etc.). For Turing, there were ultimately only purely intellectual problems to be solved – in this sense, he was the ultimate "normal psychotic," blinded for the sexual difference. Katherine Hayles is right to emphasize how the crucial intervention of the Turing test appears the moment we accept its basic dispositif, i.e. the loss of a stable embodiment, the disjunction between actually enacted and represented bodies: an irreducible gap is introduced between the "real" flesh-and-blood body behind the screen and its representation in the symbols that flicker on the computer screen.[38] Such a disjunction is co-substantial with "humanity" itself: the moment a living being starts to speak, the medium of its speech (say, voice) is minimally disembodied, in the sense that it seems to originate not in the material reality of the body that we see, but in some invisible "interiority" – a spoken word is always minimally the voice of a ventriloquist, a spectral dimension always reverberates in it. In short, one should claim that "humanity" as such ALWAYS–ALREADY WAS "posthuman" – therein resides the gist of Lacan's thesis that the symbolic order is a parasitical machine which intrudes into and supplements a human being as its artificial prosthesis.

Of course, the standard feminist question to ask here is: is this erasure of the bodily attachment gender neutral, or is it secretly gendered, so that sexual difference does not concern only the actual enacted body behind the screen, but also the different relationship between the levels of representation and enactment? Is the masculine subject in its very notion disembodied, while the feminine subject maintains the umbilical cord to its embodiment? In "The Curves of the Needle," a short essay on the gramophone from 1928,[39] Adorno notes the fundamental paradox of recording: the more the machine makes its presence known (through obtrusive noises, its clumsiness and interruptions), the stronger the experience of the actual presence of the singer – or, to put it the other way round, the more perfect the recording, the more faithfully the machine reproduces a human voice, the more humanity is removed, the stronger the effect that we are dealing with something "inauthentic".[40] This perception is to be linked to Adorno's famous "antifeminist" remark, according to which a woman's voice cannot be properly recorded because this demands the presence of her body, in contrast to a man's voice which can exert its full power as disembodied – do we not encounter here a clear case of the ideological notion of sexual difference in which man is a disembodied Spirit–Subject, while woman remains anchored in her body? However, these statements are to be read against the background of Adorno's notion of feminine hysteria as the protest of subjectivity against reification: the hysterical subject is essentially in-between, no longer fully identified with her body, not yet ready to assume the position of the disembodied speaker (or, with regard to mechanical reproduction: no longer the direct presence of the "living voice," not yet its perfect mechanical reproduction). Subjectivity is not the immediate living self-presence we attain when we shed the distorting mechanical reproduction; it is rather that remainder of "authenticity" whose traces we can discern in an imperfect mechanical reproduction. In short, the subject is something that "will have been" in its imperfect representation. Adorno's thesis thus effectively asserts feminine hysteria (and not the disembodied male voice) as the original dimension of subjectivity: in a woman's voice, the painful process of disembodiment continues to reverberate, its traces are not yet obliterated. In Kierkegaard's terms, sexual difference is the difference between "being" and "becoming": man and woman are both disembodied; however, while a man directly assumes disembodiment as an achieved state, feminine subjectivity stands for the disembodiment "in becoming."[41]

Does, then, the full formulation of the genome effectively foreclose subjectivity and/or sexual difference? When, on 26 June 2000, the completion of a "working draft" of the human genome was publicly announced, the wave of commentaries about the ethical, medical, etc. consequences of this breakthrough rendered manifest the first paradox of genome, the immediate identity of the opposite attitudes: on the one hand, the idea is that we can now formulate the very positive identity of a human being, what he or she "objectively is," what predetermines his/her development; on the other hand, knowing the complete genome – the "instruction book for human life," as it is usually described – opens up the way for the technological manipulation, enabling us to "reprogram" our (or, rather, others') bodily and psychic features. This new situation seems to signal the end of the whole series of traditional notions: theological creationism (comparing human with animal genomes makes clear that human beings evolved from animals – we share more than 99 percent of our genome with the chimpanzee), sexual reproduction (rendered superfluous by the prospect of cloning), and, ultimately, psychology or psychoanalysis – does genome not realize Freud's old dream of translating psychic processes into objective chemical processes?

Here, however, one should be attentive to the formulation which repeatedly occurs in most of the reactions to the identification of the genome: "The old adage that every disease with the exception of trauma has a genetic component is really going to be true."[42] Although this statement is meant as the assertion of a triumph, one should nonetheless focus on the exception that it concedes, the impact of a trauma. How serious and extensive is this limitation? The first thing to bear in mind here is that "trauma" is NOT simply a shorthand term for the unpredictable chaotic wealth of environmental influences, so that we are led to the standard proposition according to which the identity of a human being results from the interaction between his/her genetic inheritance and the influence of his/her environment ("nature versus nurture"). It is also not sufficient to replace this standard proposition with the more refined notion of the "embodied mind" developed by Francisco Varela:[43] a human being is not just the outcome of the interaction between genes and environment as the two opposed entities, but, rather, the engaged embodied agent who, instead of "relating" to his or her environs, mediates-creates their life-world – a bird lives in a different environment than a fish or a man . . . However, "trauma" designates a shocking encounter which, precisely, DISTURBS this immersion into one's life-world, a violent intrusion of something which doesn't fit in.

Of course, animals can also experience traumatic ruptures: is the ants' universe not thrown off the rails when a human intervention totally subverts their environs? However, the difference between animals and men is crucial here: for animals, such traumatic ruptures are the exception, they are experienced as a catastrophe which ruins their way of life; for humans, on the contrary, the traumatic encounter is a universal condition, the intrusion which sets in motion the process of "becoming human." Man is not simply overwhelmed by the impact of the traumatic encounter – as Hegel put it, but is able to "tarry with the negative," to counteract its destabilizing impact by spinning out intricate symbolic cobwebs. This is the lesson of both psychoanalysis and the Judeo–Christian tradition: the specific human vocation does not rely on the development of man's inherent potentials (on the awakening of the dormant spiritual forces OR of some genetic program); it is triggered by an external traumatic encounter, by the encounter of the Other's desire in its impenetrability. In other words (and *pace* Steve Pinker),[44] *there is no inborn "language instinct"*: there are, of course, genetic conditions that have to be met if a living being is to be able to speak; however, one actually starts to speak, one enters the symbolic universe, only in reacting to a traumatic jolt – and the mode of this reacting, i.e. the fact that, in order to cope with a trauma, we symbolize, is NOT "in our genes."

THE ANTINOMY OF CYBERSPACE REASON

The ongoing decoding of the human body and the prospect of the formulation of each individual's genome confronts us in a pressing way with the radical question of what we are: am I that, the code that can be compressed onto a single CD? Are we "nobody and nothing," just an illusion of self-awareness whose only reality is the complex interacting network of neuronal and other links? The uncanny feeling generated by playing with toys like a tamagotchi concerns the fact that we treat a virtual nonentity as an entity: we act "as if" (we believe that) there is, behind the screen, a real Self, an animal reacting to our signals, although we know well that there is nothing and nobody "behind," just the digital circuitry. However, what is even more disturbing is the implicit reflexive reversal of this insight: if there is effectively no one out there, behind the screen, *what if the same goes for myself?* What if the "I," my self-awareness, is also merely a superficial "screen" behind which there is only a "blind" complex neuronal circuit?[45] Or, to make the same point from a different perspective: why are people so afraid of air crashes? It's not the physical pain as such – what causes such horror are the two or three minutes while the plane is falling and one is fully aware that one will die shortly. Does genome identification not transpose all of us into a similar situation? That is to say, the uncanny aspect of genome identification concerns the temporal gap which separates the knowledge about what causes a certain disease from the development of the technical means to intervene and prevent this disease from evolving – the period of time in which we shall know for sure that, say, we are about to get a dangerous cancer, but will be unable to do anything to prevent it. And what about "objectively" reading our IQ or the genetic ability for other intellectual capacities? How will the awareness of this total self-objectivization affect our self-experience? The standard answer (the knowledge of our genome will enable us to intervene in our genome and change for the better our psychic and bodily properties) still begs the crucial question: if the self-objectivization is complete, who is the "I" who intervenes in "its own" genetic code in order to change it? Is this intervention itself not already objectivized in the totally scanned brain?

The "closure" anticipated by the prospect of the total scanning of the human brain does not reside only in the full correlation between the scanned neuronal activity in our brain and our subjective experience (so that a scientist will be able to give an impulse to our brain and then predict to what subjective experience this impulse will give rise), but in the much more radical notion of bypassing the very subjective experience: what it will be possible to identify through scanning will be DIRECTLY our subjective experience, so that the scientist will not even have to ask us what we experience – he will be able to READ it IMMEDIATELY on his screen.[46] On the other hand, one can argue that such a dystopian prospect involves the loop of a *petitio principii*: it silently presupposes that the same old Self which phenomenologically relies on the gap between "myself" and the objects "out there" will continue to be here after the completed self-objectivization.

The paradox, of course, is that this total self-objectivization overlaps with its opposite: what looms at the horizon of the "digital revolution" is the prospect that human beings will acquire the capacity of what Kant and other German Idealists called "intellectual intuition (*intellektuelle Anschauung*)," the closure of the gap that separates (passive) intuition and (active) production, i.e. the intuition which immediately generates the object it perceives – the capacity hitherto reserved for the infinite divine mind. On the one hand, it will be possible, through neurological implants, to switch from our "common" reality to another computer-generated reality without all the clumsy machinery of today's Virtual Reality (the awkward glasses, gloves, etc.), since the signals of virtual reality will directly reach our brain, bypassing our sensory organs:

> Your neural implants will provide the simulated sensory inputs of the virtual environment – and your virtual body – directly in your brain . . . . A typical "web site" will be a perceived virtual environment, with no external hardware required. You "go there" by mentally selecting the site and then entering that world.[47]

On the other hand, there is the complementary notion of the "Real Virtual Reality": through "nanobots" (billions of self-organizing, intelligent micro-robots), it will be possible to recreate the three-dimensional image of different realities "out there" for our "real" senses to see and enter it (the so-called "utility fog").[48] Significantly, these two opposite versions of the full virtualization of our experience of reality (direct neuronal implants versus the utility fog) mirror the difference of subjective and objective: with the utility fog, we still relate to the reality outside ourselves through our sensory experience, while the neuronal implants effectively reduce us to "brains in the vat," cutting us off from any direct perception of reality – in other words, in the first case, we "really" perceive a simulacrum of reality, while in the second case, *perception itself is simulated* through direct neuronal implants. However, in both cases, we reach a kind of omnipotence, being able to change from one to another reality by the mere power of our thoughts – to transform our bodies, the bodies of our partners, etc. etc.: "With this technology, you will be able to have almost any kind of experience with just about anyone, real or imagined, at any time."[49] The question to be asked here is: will this still be experienced as "reality"? For a human being, is "reality" not ONTOLOGICALLY defined through the minimum of RESISTANCE – real is that which resists, that which is not totally malleable to the caprices of our imagination?

As to the obvious counter-question: "However, everything cannot be virtualized – there still has to be the one 'real reality,' that of the digital or biogenetic circuitry itself which generates the very multiplicity of virtual universes!", the answer is provided by the prospect of "downloading" the entire human brain (once it is possible to scan it completely) onto an electronic machine more efficient than our awkward brains. At this crucial moment, a human being will change its ontological status "from hardware to software": it will no longer be identified with (stuck to) its material bearer (the brain in the human body). The identity of our Self is a certain neuronal pattern, the network of waves, which, in principle, can be transferred from one to another material support. Of course, there is no "pure mind," i.e. there always has to be some kind of embodiment. However, if our mind is a software pattern, it should, in principle, be possible for it to shift from one to another material support (is this not going on all the time at a different level: is the "stuff" our cells are made of not continuously changing?). The idea is that this cutting off of the umbilical cord that links us to a single body, this shift from having (and being stuck to) a *body* to freely floating between different *embodiments* will mark the true birth of the human being, relegating the entire history of humanity hitherto to the status of a confused period of transition from the animal kingdom to the true kingdom of the mind.

Here, however, philosophical–existential enigmas emerge again, and we are back at the Leibnizean problem of the identity of the indiscernibles: if (the pattern of) my brain is loaded onto a different material support, which of the two minds is "myself"? In what does the identity of "myself" consist, if it resides neither in the material support (which changes all the time) nor in the formal pattern (which can be exactly replicated)?[50] No wonder that Leibniz is one of the predominant philosophical references of the cyberspace theorists: what reverberates today is not only his dream of a universal computing machine, but the uncanny resemblance between his ontological vision of monadology and today's emerging cyberspace community in which global harmony and solipsism strangely coexist. That is to say, does our immersion into cyberspace not go hand in hand with our reduction to a Leibnizean monad which, although "without windows" that would directly open up to external reality, mirrors in itself the entire universe? Are we not more and more monads with no direct windows onto reality, interacting alone with the PC screen, encountering only the virtual simulacra, and yet immersed more than ever in the global network, synchronously communicating with the entire globe? The impasse which Leibniz tried to solve by way of introducing the notion of the "preestablished harmony" between the monads, guaranteed by God Himself, the supreme, all-encompassing monad, repeats itself today, in the guise of the problem of communication: how does each of us know that they are in touch with the "real other" behind the screen, not only with spectral simulacra? Therein resides one of the key unanswered enigmas of the Wachowski brothers' film *The Matrix*: why does the Matrix construct a *shared* virtual reality in which all humans interact? It would have been much more economic to have each human being interacting ONLY with the Matrix, so that all humans he or she were to meet would have been only digital creatures. Why? The interaction of "real" individuals through the Matrix creates its own big Other, the space of implicit meanings, surmises, etc., which can no longer be controlled by the Matrix – the Matrix is thus reduced to a mere instrument/medium, to the network that only serves as a material support for the "big Other" beyond its control.

More radically, what about the obvious Heideggerian counter-thesis that the notion of the "brain in the vat" on which this entire scenario relies, involves an ontological mistake: what accounts for the specific human dimension is not a property or pattern of the brain, but the way a human being is situated in his or her world and ex-statically relates to the things in it; language is not the relationship between an object (word) and another object (thing or thought) in the world, but the site of the historically determinate disclosure of the world-horizon as such . . . To this, one is tempted to give a cynical outright answer: OK, so what? With the immersion in virtual reality, we will effectively be deprived of the ex-static being-in-the-world that pertains to the human finitude – but what if this loss will open up to us another, unheard-of, dimension of spirituality? No wonder, then, that the old heroes of the LSD scene like Timothy Leary were so eager to embrace virtual reality: does the prospect of VR not offer the drug journey into the ethereal space of new perceptions and experiences WITHOUT direct chemical intervention in the brain, i.e. by providing from the outside, through the computer generation, the scenes that our brain itself had to create when enhanced by the drug substance?

The paradox − or, rather, the *antinomy* − of the cyberspace reason concerns precisely the fate of the body. Even advocates of cyberspace warn us that we should not totally forget our body, that we should maintain our anchoring in "real life" by returning, regularly, from our immersion in cyberspace to the intense experience of our body, from sex to jogging. We will never turn ourselves into virtual entities freely floating from one to another virtual universe: our "real life" body and its mortality is the ultimate horizon of our existence, the ultimate, innermost impossibility that underpins the immersion in all possible multiple virtual universes. Yet, at the same time, in cyberspace the body returns with a vengeance: in popular perception, "cyberspace IS hardcore pornography," i.e. hardcore pornography is perceived as the predominant use of cyberspace. The literal "enlightenment," the "lightness of being," the relief/alleviation we feel when we freely float in cyberspace (or, even more, in virtual reality), is not the experience of being bodiless, but the experience of possessing *another* − etheric, virtual, weightless − *body*, a body which does not confine us to the inert materiality and finitude, an angelic *spectral body*, a body which can be artificially recreated and manipulated. Cyberspace thus designates a turn, a kind of "negation of negation," in the gradual progress towards the disembodying of our experience (first writing instead of the "living" speech, then press, then the mass media, then radio, then TV): in cyberspace, we return to the bodily immediacy, but to an uncanny, virtual immediacy. In this sense, the claim that cyberspace contains a Gnostic dimension is fully justified: the most concise definition of Gnosticism is precisely that it is a kind of *spiritualized materialism*: its topic is not directly the higher, purely notional, reality, but a "higher" BODILY reality, a proto-reality of shadowy ghosts and undead entities.

However, the ultimate lesson of cyberspace is an even more radical one: not only do we lose our immediate material body, but we learn that there *never was* such a body – our bodily self-experience was always–already that of an imaginary constituted entity. Towards the end of his life, Heidegger conceded that, for philosophy, "the body phenomenon is the most difficult problem": "The bodily (*das Leibliche*) in the human is not something animalistic. The manner of understanding that accompanies it is something that metaphysics up till now has not touched on."[51] One is tempted to risk the hypothesis that it is precisely the psychoanalytic theory which was the first to touch on this key question: is not the Freudian eroticized body, sustained by libido, organized around erogenous zones, precisely the non-animalistic, non-biological body? Is not THIS (and not the animalistic) body the proper object of psychoanalysis?

Two

THE ANAL OBJECT

On a closer look, one can narrow this non-biological spectral body to the so-called *anal* object. Surprisingly, it was Hegel who first formulated its contours, in the chapter on "Natural Religion" in his *Phenomenology of Spirit*, where he develops the notion of the religion of the artificer (*Kunstmeister*), in which Natural Religion culminates and points towards its own sublation: after the notion of God as Light and the celebration of plant and animal as divine, where the object of veneration is something *found* in nature, subjects start to *produce themselves* the objects they honor (Egyptian pyramids and obelisks).[1] This artificer is to be opposed to the Ancient Greek *artist* (*Kuenstler*). An "artificer" is an artisan who is characterized by the two opposite features: in contrast to the artist's free subjectivity, his creativity is "blind" compulsion, epitomized by the Ancient Egyptian scene of tens of thousands people engaged in the building of the pyramid, performing it as "an instinctive operation, like the building of a honeycomb by bees";[2] on the other hand, in contrast to the artist's organic spontaneity, the artificer's work is "reflected," effort, not spontaneous outgrowth.

The artificer still struggles with the material, unable to achieve the direct expression of the Spirit in it. We do not have a meaning proper, expressed in articulate speech, but an infinite longing for meaning which remains a mystery, a riddle not only to us, but to the Ancient Egyptians themselves. The Greeks were the true artists, practising the direct expression of the spirit in the organic form; the space for this direct harmonious expression emerged after Oedipus solved the riddle of the Sphinx. In contrast to it, Egyptian art doesn't yet properly *speak*: its speech is encoded in hieroglyphs, in the pseudo-concrete forms, not yet the abstract alphabetic letters. Here follows Hegel's well-known endlessly quoted analysis: Sphinx as half-man half-animal, as the Spirit not yet liberated from its material constraint. Within this horizon, man as such appears only as and in a tomb, as the empty place for the dead body, not as a living subjectivity:

> Therefore the work, even when it is wholly purged of the animal element and wears only the shape of self-consciousness, is still the soundless shape which needs the rays of the rising sun in order to have sound which, generated by light, is even then merely noise and not speech, and reveals only an outer, not the inner, self.[3]

Here – as well as later, in his *Lectures on Aesthetics* – Hegel refers to the ancient Egyptian sacred statue which, at every sunset, as if by a miracle, issued a deeply reverberating sound. This mysterious sound magically resonating from within an inanimate object is the best metaphor for the birth of subjectivity, for subjectivity in its proto-ontological status. Subjectivity is here reduced to a spectral voice, a voice in which resonates not the self-presence of a living subject, but the void of its absence. What we have to renounce is thus the commonsense notion of a primordial, fully constituted reality in which sight and sound harmoniously complement each other: an unbridgeable gap separates forever a human body from "its" voice. The voice displays a spectral autonomy, it never quite belongs to the body we see, so that even when we see a living person talking, there is always a minimum of ventriloquism at work: it is as if the speaker's own voice hollows him out and in a sense speaks "by itself," through him. What this means is that we must be careful here not to miss the tension, the antagonism, between the *silent* scream and the vibrant tone, i.e., the moment when this silent scream *resounds*. The true object-voice is mute, "stuck in the throat," and what effectively reverberates is the void: resonance always takes place *in a vacuum* – the tone as such is originally the lament for the lost object. This resonance is thus not the secondary degradation of a "natural" speech: it takes place BEFORE the emergence of the "full" speaking subject. Usually, Hegel's notion of the Ancient Greek universe is interpreted as the reference to the lost organic, harmonious Whole, which is then destroyed by the work of negativity – what we get here is the PREHISTORY of the Greek harmonious Whole, the spectral past that haunts it. (Is, then, the Greek Religion of Art a solution to the Egyptian riddle? Definitely not: the reflexive excess reappears in it with a vengeance – the very fact that the person who resolves the riddle is Oedipus should be sufficient to dispel any notion of a happy outcome.)

There is yet another, even stranger reflexive twist to Hegel's argument. In Egyptian religious artistry, consciousness struggles to express itself but its expression fails, the gap remains between the inner being and its external expression, which is a mere "unessential husk," a "covering for the inner being."[4] In order for this inner being to persist in its failed expression, this very gap between the inner being and its inadequate husk must be reflexively inscribed in external objective reality, in the guise of an external object in which the inner being acquires direct existence – and this inner being is, in the first instance, "still simple darkness, the unmoved, the black, formless stone" ("die einfache Finsternis, das Unbewegte, der schwarze formlose Stein)."[5] (This new version of the "spirit is a bone" theme, of course, anachronistically refers to the Black Stone in the Kaaba in Mecca, the dark formless meteorite elevated into the sacred object of Islam.)

The anal association is here fully justified: the immediate appearance of the Inner is formless shit.[6] The small child who gives his shit as a present is in a way giving the immediate equivalent of his Inner Self. Freud's well-known identification of excrement as the primordial form of gift, of an innermost object that the small child gives to its parents, is thus not as naive as it may appear: the often-overlooked point is that this piece of myself offered to the Other radically oscillates between the Sublime and – not the Ridiculous, but, precisely – the excremental.[7] This is the reason why, for Lacan, one of the features which distinguishes man from animals is that, with humans, the disposal of shit becomes a problem: not because it has a bad smell, but because it came out from our innermost selves. We are ashamed of shit because, in it, we expose/externalize our innermost intimacy. Animals do not have a problem with it because they do not have an "interior" like humans. One should refer here to Otto Weininger, who designated volcanic lava as "the shit of the earth" ("Die Lava ist der Dreck der Erde)."[8] It comes from inside the body, and this inside is evil, criminal: "The Inner of the body is very criminal. (Das Innere des Koerpers ist sehr verbrecherisch.)"[9] Here we encounter the same speculative ambiguity as with the penis, organ of urination and procreativity: when our innermost self is directly externalized, the result is disgusting.

This self-exposure is gaining hitherto inconceivable dimensions: a quick search on the web will reveal sites where you can watch what the mini-camera at the top of a dildo sees when it penetrates the vagina or sites connected to a camera inside a toilet bowl, so that you can observe from below women defecating and urinating. If there ever was an exemplary case of what Hegel, in his *Phenomenology of Spirit*, called the "topsy-turvy world (*die verkehrte Welt*)," it is the remarkable scene from Bunuel's *Le Fantôme de la liberté*, in which relations between eating and excreting are inverted: people sit at their toilets around the table, pleasantly talking, and when one of them wants to eat, he silently asks the housekeeper "Where is that place, you know?" and sneaks away to a small room in the back. This scene involves a dialectic much more complex than the commonplace about how the opposition between public decency and private obscenity is ultimately arbitrary and can be turned around – its message to the spectator is: "In your everyday life, you think: 'True, man is an animal who does detestable things like excreting shit, but we should not forget that he nonetheless does noble things, like elevating the act of eating (which produces shit) into a sublime social ritual.' However, your true stance is: "True, man does some really enjoyable things like relieving himself in the toilet, but nonetheless, we should not forget that he has to pay for this by the boring civilized ritual of eating." (The true stance is *this one* and not, as one would expect: "True, man is able to elevate even the animal function of eating into a sublime ritual, but let us not forget that, ultimately, he does have to accomplish the vulgar act of going to the toilet.")

Vladimir Sorokin's extraordinary "postmodern" novel

Norma (1994 – in Russian, the title means "norm," also in the sense of the "production norm," i.e. the amount of work to be accomplished in a given period of time) displays a deep insight into the working of the anal object. Each chapter is written as a pastiche of some classic or modern prototype. One of them reports on the legendary meeting, in the early 1960s, between Alexander Solzhenytsin and Konstantin Tvardovsky, the editor-in-chief of *Novy Mir*, the journal which first serialized Solzhenytsin's *One Day in the Life of Ivan Denisovich*; when Solzhenytsin enters Tvardovsky's office, Tvardovsky approaches him and asks him confidently "Do you have IT? You know, the norm . . ."; after Solzhenytsin says "Yes!", Tvardovsky utters a deeply satisfied "Oooh, yes . . ." Another chapter, perfectly mocking the heroic style of Soviet World War II novels, reports on two Russian soldiers in a trench, under attack by the Germans – when one of them is hit, he cries to his comrade: "But what about the norm, I haven't yet delivered it . . ."; etc. etc., until, at the end, we finally learn what this mysterious "norm" is – shit itself. Shit is thus the name for the formless "thing in itself," for that which remains the same in all possible symbolic universes, within which it can assume different guises of a precious object – the dissident manuscript, the last letter to one's nearest . . .

This externalized shit is precisely the equivalent of the alien monster that colonizes the human body, penetrating it and dominating it from within, and which, at the climactic moment of a science-fiction horror movie, breaks out of the body through the mouth or directly through the chest. Perhaps even more exemplary than Ridley Scott's *Alien* here is Jack Sholder's *Hidden*, in which the worm-like alien creature forced out of the body at the film's end directly evokes anal associations (a gigantic piece of shit, since the alien compels humans penetrated by it to eat voraciously and belch in an embarrassingly disgusting way).

In a further analysis, one should here oppose this externalized INNER object (shit) as the subject's direct equivalent, to the opposite, EXTERNAL, mode of domination: the notion of a MASK as the Evil Object which has a life of its own and takes over the subject who puts it on his face – all of a sudden, after he puts the mask on, the subject is caught in an inexplicable compulsion. Recall *Liar, Liar* with Jim Carrey, a film which, like his earlier work *The Mask*, focuses on an ex-timate (externally imposed, but echoing the innermost drive) absolute compulsion: in *The Mask*, it is the compulsion to enjoy, to act as a maniac cartoon-like character, once the mask takes possession of the hero; in *Liar, Liar*, it is the compulsion contracted by a lawyer through the promise to his son to tell the truth and nothing but the truth for 24 hours. The homology is uncanny: in both cases, giving way to our innermost self is experienced by the subject as being colonized by some parasitic foreign intruder which takes possession of him against his will, somewhat like when we are haunted by a vulgar popular melody – no matter how we fight it, we ultimately succumb to it, to its mimetic power, and start to move along to its stupid rhythm . . .

Jim Carrey is best known for his "making faces," for the ridiculously exaggerated facial contortions which render his desperate resistance to the colonizing compulsion of the external drive. It would be worthwhile to compare his "making faces" with another actor's (and director's) "making faces," that of Jerry Lewis. Perhaps the key moment in a Jerry Lewis film occurs when the idiot he plays is compelled to become aware of the havoc his behavior has caused: at that moment, when he is stared at by all the people around him, unable to sustain their gaze, he engages in his unique mode of making faces, of ridiculously disfiguring his facial expression, combined with twisting his hands and rolling his eyes. This desperate attempt of the embarrassed subject to *efface* his presence, to erase himself from others' view, is to be opposed to Carrey's "making faces," which functions in an almost exactly opposite way – as a desperate attempt to *assert* one's presence.

The uncanny feature is here the very parallel between *jouissance* and truth, between the compulsion-to-enjoy and the compulsion to tell the truth, which means that truth itself can function in the mode of the Real. Does this parallel not recall the strange fact, noted long ago by Lacan, that Freud uses exactly the same words to designate the insistence of drive and of reason: in both cases, their voice is low and slow, but it persists and makes itself heard? Even such a radical stance as that of Buddhism is here not sufficient – to quote the Dalai Lama himself, the beginning of wisdom is "to realize that all living beings are equal in not wanting unhappiness and suffering and equal in the right to rid themselves of suffering."[10] The Freudian drive designates precisely the paradox of "wanting unhappiness," of finding excessive pleasure in suffering itself.

What the two opposite modes (the inner formless body dominating the subject and the external compulsion) have in common is their COMPULSORY nature: in both cases, either as the externally imposed mask or as the internal formless object, the Thing deprives the subject of his autonomy, acting as a compulsion that turns him into a helpless puppet.

Nowhere is this overlapping of the Sublime and the Excremental more evident than apropos of Tibet, one of the central references of the post-Christian "spiritual" imaginary. Today, Tibet increasingly plays the role of such a fantasmatic Thing (the fantasy formation to which we refer when we talk about Tibet), of a jewel which, when one approaches it too much, turns into the excremental object. It is a commonplace to claim that the fascination exerted by Tibet on the Western imagination, especially on the broad public in the USA, provides an exemplary case of the "colonization of the imaginary": it reduces the actual Tibet to a screen for the projection of Western ideological fantasies. The very inconsistency of this image of Tibet, with its direct coincidences of opposites, seems to bear witness to its fantasmatic status. Tibetans are portrayed as people leading a simple life of spiritual satisfaction, fully accepting their fate, liberated from the excessive craving of the Western subject who is always searching for more, AND as a bunch of filthy, cheating, cruel, sexually promiscuous primitives. Lhasa itself becomes a version of Franz Kafka's Castle: sublime and majestic when first seen from afar, but then changing into the "paradise of filth," a gigantic pile of shit, as soon as one actually enters the city. Potala, the central palace towering over Lhasa, is a kind of heavenly residence on earth, magically floating in the air, AND a labyrinth of stale seedy rooms and corridors full of monks engaged in obscure magic rituals, including sexual perversions. The social order is presented as the model of organic harmony, AND as the tyranny of the cruel corrupted theocracy keeping ordinary people ignorant. Tibetan Buddhism itself is simultaneously hailed as the most spiritual of all religions, the last shelter of the ancient Wisdom, AND as the utmost primitive superstition, relying on prayer wheels and similar cheap magic tricks . . . This oscillation between jewel and shit is not the oscillation BETWEEN the idealized ethereal fantasy and the raw reality: in such an oscillation, BOTH extremes are fantasmatic, i.e. the fantasmatic space is the very space of this immediate passage from one extreme to the other.

The first antidote against this topos of the raped jewel, of the isolated place of people who just wanted to be left alone, but were repeatedly penetrated by foreigners, is to remind ourselves that Tibet was already IN ITSELF an antagonistic, split society, not an organic Whole whose harmony was disturbed only by external intruders. Tibetan unity and independence were imposed from the outside: Tibet emerged as a unified country, in a form which lasted till 1950, in the ninth century, when it established a "patron–priest" relationship with the Mongols: the Mongols protected the Tibetans, who in turn provided spiritual guidance to Mongolia. (The very name "Dalai Lama" is of Mongol origin and was conferred on Tibetan religious leader by the Mongols.) Events took the same turn in the seventeenth century, when the Fifth Lama, the greatest of them all – again, through the benevolent foreign patronage – established the Tibet we know today, starting the construction of Potala. What followed was the long tradition of factional struggles, in which, as a rule, the winners won by inviting foreigners (Mongols, Chinese) to intervene. This story culminates in the recent partial shift of the Chinese strategy: rather than sheer military coercion, they now rely on ethnic and economic colonization, rapidly transforming Lhasa into a Chinese version of the capitalist Wild West, with karaoke bars intermingled with Disney-like "Buddhist theme parks" for Western tourists. In short, what the media image of the brutal Chinese soldiers and policemen terrorizing the Buddhist monks conceals is the much more effective American-style socio-economic transformation: in a decade or two, Tibetans will be reduced to the status of the Native Americans in the USA.

The second antidote is therefore the opposite one: to denounce the split nature of the Western image of Tibet as a "reflexive determination" of the split attitude of the West itself, combining violent penetration and respectful sacralization. Colonel Francis Younghusband, who in 1904 led the English regiment of 1200 men that penetrated to Lhasa and forced the trade agreement on the Tibetans – a true precursor of the late Chinese invasion – mercilessly ordered the slaughter by machine gun of hundreds of Tibetan soldiers who were armed only with swords and lances and thus forced his way to Lhasa. However, this same person experienced a true epiphany in his last day in Lhasa: "Never again could I think of evil, or ever again be at enmity with any man. All nature and all humanity were bathed in a rosy glowing radiancy; and life for the future seemed nought but buoyancy and light."[11] The same went for his commander-in-chief, the infamous Lord Curzon, who justified Younghusband's expedition: "The Tibetans are a weak and cowardly people, their very pusillanimity rendering them readily submissive to any powerful military authority who entering their country should forthwith give a sharp lesson and a wholesome dread of offending."[12] Yet this same Curzon who insisted "nothing can or will be done with the Tibetans until they are frightened," declared in a speech at an Old Etonian banquet:

> The East is a university in which the scholar never takes his degree. It is a temple where the supplicant adores but never catches sight of the object of his devotion. It is a journey the goal of which is always in sight but is never attained.[13]

What was and is ABSOLUTELY foreign to Tibet is this Western logic of desire to penetrate the inaccessible object beyond a limit, through a great ordeal, against natural obstacles and vigilant patrols. In his travelogue *To Lhasa in Disguise*, published in 1924, William McGovern

> raised the tantalizing question: What provokes a man to risk so much on such an arduous, dangerous, and unnecessary journey to a place that is so manifestly unappealing when he at last gets there? To the Tibetans, at least, such a useless trek seemed nonsensical. McGovern wrote of his efforts to explain his motives to an incredulous Tibetan official in Lhasa: "It was impossible to get him to understand the pleasures of undertaking an adventure and dangerous journey. Had I talked about anthropological research he would have thought me mad."[14]

The lesson to our followers of Tibetan Wisdom is thus that, if we want to be Tibetans, we should forget about Tibet and do it HERE. Therein resides the ultimate paradox: the more Europeans try to penetrate the "true" Tibet, the more the very FORM of their endeavor undermines their goal. We should appreciate the full scope of this paradox, especially with regard to "Eurocentrism." The Tibetans were extremely self-centered: "To them, Tibet was the center of the world, the heart of civilization."[15] What characterizes the European civilization is, on the contrary, precisely its *ex-centered* character – the notion that the ultimate pillar of Wisdom, the secret *agalma*, the spiritual treasure, the lost object–cause of desire, which we in the West long ago betrayed, could be recuperated out there, in the forbidden exotic place. Colonization was never simply the imposition of Western values, the assimilation of the Oriental and other Others to the European

Sameness; it was always also the search for the lost spiritual innocence of OUR OWN civilization. This story begins at the very dawn of Western civilization, in Ancient Greece: for the Greeks, Egypt was just such a mythic place of the lost ancient wisdom.

The same holds today in our own societies: the difference between authentic fundamentalists and the "moral majority" perverted fundamentalists is that the first (for example, the Amish in the USA) get along very well with their American neighbors because they are centered on their own world, not bothered by what goes on out there, among "them," while the moral majority fundamentalist is always haunted by the ambiguous attitude of horror/envy with regard to the unspeakable pleasures in which sinners engage. The reference to envy as one of the seven deadly sins can thus serve as a perfect instrument enabling us to distinguish the authentic fundamentalism from its moral majority mockery: authentic fundamentalists DO NOT ENVY their neighbors their different *jouissance*.[16] Envy is grounded in what one is tempted to call the "transcendental illusion" of desire, strictly correlative to the Kantian transcendental illusion: a natural "propensity" in the human being to (mis)perceive the object which gives body to the primordial lack as object which is lacking, which was lost (and, consequently, possessed prior to this loss); this illusion sustains the longing to regain the lost object, as if this object has a positive substantial identity independently of its being lost.

SACRIFICE VERSUS THE FEMININE RENUNCIATION

The conclusion to be drawn from this is a simple and radical one: moral majority fundamentalists and tolerant multi-culturalists are the two sides of the same coin, they both share the fascination with the Other. In moral majority, this fascination displays the envious hatred of the Other's excessive *jouissance*, while the multiculturalist tolerance of the Other's Otherness is also more twisted than it may appear – it is sustained by a secret desire for the Other to REMAIN "other," not to become too much like us. In contrast to both these positions, the only TRULY tolerant attitude towards the Other is that of the authentic radical fundamentalist.

This, perhaps, is the only true lesson we, Westerners, can get from the unfortunate Tibet: the superfluous and fake character of the compulsion to *sacrifice*. In order to obtain the Thing, we do NOT have first to construct the scenario of its loss, of the Thing being snatched from us by the Other, or of us betraying the Thing. What, then, is the sacrifice? What is a priori false about it? At its most elementary, sacrifice relies on the notion of exchange: I offer to the Other something precious to me in order to get back from the Other something even more vital to me (the "primitive" tribes sacrifice animals or even humans so that Gods will repay them by enough rainfall, military victory, etc.). The next, already more intricate, level is to conceive sacrifice as a gesture which does not directly aim at some profitable exchange with the Other to whom we sacrifice: its more basic aim is rather to ascertain that there IS some Other out there who is able to reply (or not) to our sacrificial entreaties. Even if the Other does not grant my wish, I can at least be assured that there IS an Other who, maybe, next time will respond differently: the world out there, inclusive of all catastrophes that may befall me, is not a meaningless blind machinery, but a partner in a possible dialogue, so that even a catastrophic outcome is to be read as a meaningful response, not as a kingdom of blind chance . . . Lacan here goes a step further: the notion of sacrifice usually associated with Lacanian psychoanalysis is that of a gesture that enacts the disavowal of the impotence of the big Other: at its most elementary, the subject does not offer his sacrifice to profit from it himself, but to fill in the lack in the Other, to sustain the appearance of the Other's omnipotence or, at least, consistency.

Let us recall *Beau Geste*, the classic Hollywood adventure melodrama from 1938, in which the eldest of the three brothers (Gary Cooper) who live with their benevolent aunt, in what seems to be a gesture of excessive ungrateful cruelty, steals the enormously expensive diamond necklace which is the pride of the aunt's family, and disappears with it, knowing that his reputation is ruined, that he will be forever known as the ungracious embezzler of his benefactress – so why did he do it? At the end of the film, we learn that he did it in order to prevent the embarrassing disclosure that the necklace was a fake: unbeknownst to all others, he knew that, some time ago, the aunt had to sell the necklace to a rich maharaja in order to save the family from bankruptcy, and replaced it with a worthless imitation. Just prior to his "theft," he learned that a distant uncle who co-owned the necklace wanted it sold for financial gain; if the necklace were to be sold, the fact that it is a fake would undoubtedly be discovered, so the only way to retain the aunt's and thus the family's honor is to stage its theft . . .

This is the proper deception of the crime of stealing: to occlude the fact that, ultimately, THERE IS NOTHING TO STEAL – in this way, the constitutive lack of the Other is concealed, i.e. the illusion is maintained that the Other possessed what was stolen from it. If, in love, one gives what one doesn't possess, in a crime of love, one steals from the beloved Other what the Other doesn't possess . . . to this alludes the "beau geste" of the film's title. And therein resides also the meaning of sacrifice: one sacrifices oneself (one's honor and future in respectful society) to maintain the appearance of the Other's honor, to save the beloved Other from shame.

However, Lacan's rejection of sacrifice as inauthentic locates the falsity of the sacrificial gesture also in another, much more uncanny dimension. Let us take the example of Jeannot Szwarc's *Enigma* (1981), one of the better variations on what is arguably the basic matrix of cold war spy thrillers with artistic pretensions á la John le Carré (an agent is sent into the cold to accomplish a mission; when, in enemy territory, he is betrayed and captured, it dawns on him that he was sacrificed, i.e. that the failure of his mission was from the very beginning planned by his superiors in order to achieve the true goal of the operation – say, to keep secret the identity of the true mole of the West in the KGB apparatus . . .). *Enigma* tells the story of a dissident journalist-turned-spy who emigrates to the West and is then recruited by the CIA and sent to East Germany to get hold of a scrambling/descrambling computer chip whose possession enables the owner to read all communications between KGB headquarters and its outposts. However, small signs tell the spy that there is something wrong with his mission, i.e. that East Germans and Russians were already in advance informed about his arrival – so what is going on? Is it that the Communists have a mole in the CIA headquarters who informed them of this secret mission? As we learn towards the film's end, the solution is much more ingenious: the CIA *already possesses* the scrambling chip, but, unfortunately, the Russians suspect this fact, and have temporarily stopped using this computer network for their secret communications. The true aim of the operation was the attempt by the CIA to convince the Russians that they do not possess the chip: they sent an agent to get it and, at the same time, deliberately let the Russians know that there is an operation going on to get the chip; of course, the CIA counts on the fact that the Russians will arrest the agent. The ultimate result will thus be that, by successfully preventing the mission, the Russians will be convinced that the Americans do not possess it and that it is therefore safe to use this communication link . . . The tragic aspect of the story, of course, is that the mission's failure is taken into account: the CIA *wants* the mission to fail, i.e. the poor dissident agent is sacrificed in advance for the higher goal of convincing the opponent that one doesn't possess his secret.

The strategy here is to stage a search operation in order to convince the Other (the enemy) that one does not already possess what one is looking for – in short, one feigns a lack, a want, in order to conceal from the Other that one already possesses the *agalma*, the Other's innermost secret. This structure is somehow connected with the basic paradox of symbolic castration as constitutive of desire, in which the object has to be lost in order to be regained on the inverse ladder of desire regulated by the Law. Symbolic castration is usually defined as the loss of something that one never possessed, i.e. the object–cause of desire is an object which emerges through the very gesture of its loss/withdrawal; however, what we encounter here, in the case of *Enigma*, is the obverse structure of feigning a loss. Insofar as the Other of the symbolic Law prohibits *jouissance*, the only way for the subject to enjoy is to feign that he lacks the object that provides *jouissance*, i.e. to conceal from the Other's gaze its possession by way of staging the spectacle of the desperate search for it.

This also casts a new light on the topic of sacrifice: one

sacrifices not in order to get something from the Other, but in order to dupe the Other, in order to convince him/it that one is still missing something, i.e. *jouissance*. This is why obsessionals repeatedly experience the compulsion to accomplish their compulsive rituals of sacrifice – in order to disavow their *jouissance* in the eyes of the Other. At a different level, does the same not hold for the so-called "woman's sacrifice," for the woman adopting the role of remaining in shadow and sacrificing herself for her husband or family? Is this sacrifice not also false in the sense of serving to dupe the Other, of convincing it that, through the sacrifice, the woman is effectively desperately craving something that she lacks? In this precise sense, sacrifice and castration are to be opposed: far from involving the voluntary acceptance of castration, sacrifice is the most refined way of disavowing it, i.e. of acting as if one effectively possessed the hidden treasure that made me an object worthy of love . . . [17]

In his unpublished Seminar on Anxiety (1962/3, lesson of December 5 1962), Lacan emphasizes the way the hysteric's anxiety relates to the fundamental lack in the Other which makes the Other inconsistent/barred: a hysteric perceives the lack in the Other, its impotence, inconsistency, fake, but he is not ready to sacrifice the part of himself that would complete the Other, fill in its lack – this refusal to sacrifice sustains the hysteric's eternal complaint that the Other will somehow manipulate and exploit him, use him, deprive him of his most precious possession . . . More precisely, this does not mean that the hysteric disavows his castration: the hysteric (neurotic) does not hold back from his castration (he is not a psychotic or a pervert, i.e. he fully accepts his castration); he merely does not want to "functionalize" it, to put it in the service of the Other, i.e. what he holds back from is "making his castration into what the Other is lacking, that is to say, into something positive that is the guarantee of this function of the Other." (In contrast to the hysteric, the pervert readily assumes this role of sacrificing himself, i.e. of serving as the object-instrument that fills in the Other's lack – as Lacan puts it, the pervert "offers himself loyally to the Other's *jouissance*".) The falsity of sacrifice resides in its underlying presupposition, which is that I effectively possess, hold in me, the precious ingredient coveted by the Other and promising to fill in its lack. On a closer view, of course, the hysteric's refusal appears in all its ambiguity: I refuse to sacrifice the *agalma* in me BECAUSE THERE IS NOTHING TO SACRIFICE, because I am unable to fill in your lack.[18]

One should always bear in mind that, for Lacan, the ultimate aim of psychoanalysis is not to enable the subject to assume the necessary sacrifice (to "accept symbolic castration," to renounce immature narcissistic attachments, etc.), but to *resist* the terrible attraction of sacrifice – attraction which, of course, is none other than that of the superego. Sacrifice is ultimately the gesture by means of which we aim at compensating the guilt imposed by the impossible superego injunction (the "obscure gods" evoked by Lacan are another name for the superego). It is therefore all the more crucial not to confuse the logic of "irrational" sacrifice aimed at redeeming or saving the Other (or at deceiving him, which ultimately amounts to the same) with another type of renunciation paradigmatic of the feminine heroines in modern-age literature – a tradition whose exemplary cases are those of Princess de Clèves and Isabel Archer. In Madame de Lafayette's *The Princesse de Clèves*, the answer to the enigma "Why, after her husband's death, doesn't the Princess marry the Duke of Nemours, although they are both passionately in love with each other, and there are no legal or moral obstacles to it?" is twofold. First, the memory of her good and loving husband who died because of her love for the Duke, i.e. who was not able to withstand the torment of jealousy when he thought that his wife and the Duke had spent two nights together: for her, the only way not to betray her husband's memory is to avoid any liaison with the Duke. However, as she openly admits to the Duke in the long traumatic conversation which concludes the novel, this reason would not be in itself sufficient and strong enough if it were not sustained by another fear and apprehension, by the awareness of the transitory nature of male love:

> What I feel I owe to the memory of M. de Clèves would be weak if it were not supported by the cause of my own peace of mind, and the arguments in favour of that must be sustained by those of duty.[19]

She is well aware that the Duke's love for her was so enduring and firm *because* it did not find a quick gratification, i.e. because the obstacles to it were insurmountable; if they were to marry, his love would probably pass, he would be seduced by other women, and the thought of these future torments is unbearable to her. So, precisely in order to maintain the absolute and eternal character of their love, they must remain separated and thus avoid the "way of all flesh," the degradation which comes with time. After her desperate cry "Why has fate put such an insurmountable barrier between us?", the Duke answers with a reproach: "There is no barrier, Madame. You alone stand in the way of my happiness; you alone are subjecting yourself to a law, to which neither morality nor reason can subject you." To that she answers: "It is true that I am sacrificing much to an idea of duty that exists only in my mind."[20] We have here the opposition between the simple external obstacles which thwart our desires and the internal, inherent obstacle constitutive of desire as such, or, in Lacanese, between the law qua external regulation of our needs and the Law which is the inherent obverse, the constituent of, and thus ultimately identical to desire itself.

Crucial is here the elementary structure of "overdetermination," i.e. the fact that the Princess obeys two reasons in her decision not to marry her love: the first (moral) reason can only prevail insofar as it is supported by the second reason (of "inner peace," of avoiding the torments which lie ahead). In the antagonistic tension between *jouissance* and pleasure, the symbolic Law is on the side of the pleasure principle, it functions as a barrier against the traumatic encounters of the Real which would disturb the precarious balance of pleasure. In this precise sense, Lacan claims that the symbolic Law only elevates into a prohibition the quasi-natural obstacle to the full satisfaction of desire:

> . . . it is not the Law itself that bars the subject's access to *jouissance* – rather it creates out of an almost natural barrier a barred subject. For it is pleasure that sets the limits on *jouissance*, pleasure as that which binds incoherent life together.[21]

In the case of the unfortunate Princess de Clèves, this predominance of the pleasure principle is clearly signalled by her reference to the concern for her "inner peace" as the true reason for her rejection to marry the Duke: she prefers "inner peace," i.e. the life of balance, of homeostasis, to the painful turmoil of passionate love; the injunction which prevents her from marrying the Duke on behalf of the memory of her deceased husband elevated this "natural barrier" of pleasure principle into a moral prohibition. This predicament of the Princesse de Clèves also enables us to grasp Lacan's proposition according to which "desire is a defence, a prohibition against going beyond a certain limit in *jouissance*"[22]: the prohibition (to marry the Duke) which sustains her desire for him and eternalizes it, elevating it into an absolute, is a defence against the painful turmoil of excessive *jouissance* of the consummated relationship with him. The true Law/ Prohibition is thus not imposed "by virtue and reason," i.e. by an agency external to itself, but by desire itself – Law IS desire.

Another way to arrive at the same conclusion is to take into account the fact that, in a fictional narrative, the repressed truth is as a rule articulated in the guise of a "story within a story", as in Goethe's *Elective Affinities*, where the proper ethical attitude of "not compromising one's desire," is articulated in the story about two youthful lovers from a small village, told by a visitor to the mansion. In *The Princesse de Clèves*, this truth is articulated in the guise of the story narrated to Princess de Clèves by her husband: his best friend Sancerre was first devastated by the sudden death of Madame de Tournon, his great love. However, an even worse experience awaits him when, after mourning the idealized Madame, he suddenly discovers that she was unfaithful to him in a very calculating way. This tragic predicament, this "second death," the death of the (lost) ideal itself, is what the unfortunate Princess wants to avoid. In short, her predicament is that of a forced choice: if she renounces marrying the Duke, she will at least gain and retain him "in eternity" (Kierkegaard) as her only and true love; if she marries him, she will sooner or later lose both, his bodily proximity as well as his eternal passionate attachment to her.

However, these two reasons for not marrying her love do not cover the entire field. One is tempted to claim that the Princess enumerates them in order to conceal the third, perhaps the crucial one: the *jouissance*, the satisfaction brought about by the very act of renunciation, of maintaining the distance towards the beloved object. This paradoxical *jouissance* characterizes the movement of drive as that which finds satisfaction in circulating around the object and repeatedly missing it. The three reasons thus refer to the triad of IRS: the *symbolic* moral prohibition, the *imaginary* concern for the balance of pleasures, the *real* of drive. One should interpret the other great mysterious feminine "No!", that of Isabel Archer at the end of Henry James's *The Portrait of a Lady*, along these same lines. Why doesn't Isabel leave Osmond, although she definitely doesn't love him and is fully aware of his manipulations? The reason is not the moral pressure exerted on her by the notion of what is expected of a woman in her position – Isabel has sufficiently proven that, when she wants, she is quite willing to override conventions: "Isabel stays because of her commitment to the bond of her word, and she stays because she is unwilling to abandon what she still sees as a decision made out of her sense of independence."[23] In short, as Lacan put it apropos of Sygne de Coufontaine in Claudel's *The Hostage*, Isabel is also "the hostage of the word." So it is wrong to interpret this act as a sacrifice bearing witness to the proverbial "feminine masochism": although Isabel was obviously manipulated into marrying Osmond, her act was her own, and to leave Osmond would simply equal depriving herself of her autonomy.[24] While men sacrifice themselves for a *Thing* (country, freedom, honor), only women are able to sacrifice themselves for *nothing*. (Or: men are moral, while only women are properly ethical.)

THE REAL OF THE (CHRISTIAN) ILLUSION

It is our contention that this "empty" sacrifice is the Christian gesture par excellence: it is only against the background of this empty gesture that one can begin to appreciate the uniqueness of the figure of Christ. Let us start with Gilles Deleuze's exemplary analysis of Chaplin's late films:

> Between the small Jewish barber and the dictator (in *The Great Dictator*), the difference is as negligable as that between their respective moustaches. Yet it results in two situations as infinitely remote, as far opposed as those of victim and executioner. Likewise, in *Monsieur Verdoux*, the difference between the two aspects or demeanors of the same man, the lady-assassin and the loving husband of a paralyzed wife, is so thin that all his wife's intuition is required for the premonition that somehow he "changed." . . . the burning question of *Limelight* is: what is that "nothing," that sign of age, that small difference of triteness, on account of which the funny clown's number changes into a tedious spectacle?[25]

The paradigmatic case of this imperceptible "almost nothing" are the old paranoiac science-fiction films from the early 1950s about aliens occupying a small American town: they look and act like normal Americans, we can distinguish them only via the reference to some minor detail. It is Ernst Lubitsch's *To Be Or Not To Be* which brings this logic to its dialectical climax. In one of the funniest scenes of the film, the pretentious Polish actor who as part of a secret mission has to impersonate the cruel senior Gestapo officer Erhardt, does this impersonation in an exaggerated way, reacting to the remarks of his interlocutor about his cruel treatment of the Poles with loud vulgar laughter and a satisfied awareness,

"So they call me Concentration Camp Erhardt, hahaha!" We, the spectators, take this for a ridiculous caricature – however, when, later in the film, the REAL Erhardt appears, he reacts to his interlocutors in *exactly the same way*. Although the "real" Erhardt thus in a way imitates his imitation, "plays himself," this uncanny coincidence makes all the more palpable the absolute gap that separates him from the poor Polish impersonator. In Hitchcock's *Vertigo*, we find a more tragic version of the same uncanny coincidence: the low-class Judy who, under the pressure exerted from and out of her love for Scottie, endeavors to look and act like the high-class fatal and ethereal Madeleine, turns out to BE Madeleine: they are the same person, since the "true" Madeleine Scottie encountered was already a fake. However, this identity of Judy and Judy–Madeleine, this difference between the two fakes, again renders all the more palpable the absolute otherness of Madeleine with regard to Judy – the Madeleine that is given nowhere, that is present just in the guise of the ethereal "aura" that envelops Judy–Madeleine. The Real is the appearance as appearance, it not only appears WITHIN appearances, but it is also NOTHING BUT its own appearance – it is just a certain GRIMACE of reality, a certain imperceptible, unfathomable, ultimately illusory feature that accounts for the absolute difference within the identity.

So, with regard to the grimace of real/reality, it is crucial to keep open the reversibility of this formulation. In a first approach, reality is a grimace of the real – the real, structured/distorted into the "grimace" we call reality through the pacifying symbolic network, somehow like the Kantian *Ding-an-sich* (thing-in-itself) structured into what we experience as objective reality through the transcendental network. In a second, deeper, approach, things appear exactly the same as in a first approach – with, however, a little twist: the real itself is nothing but a grimace of reality, i.e. the obstacle, the "bone in the throat" which forever distorts our perception of reality, introducing anamorphic stains in it, or the pure *Schein* (appearing) of Nothing that only "shines through" reality, since it is "in itself" thoroughly without substance.[26]

A homologous inversion is to be accomplished apropos of the "illusion of the real," of the postmodern denouncing every (effect of) the Real as an illusion: what Lacan opposes to it is the much more subversive notion of the *Real of the illusion itself*.[27] Consider the fashionable argument according to which Real Socialism failed because it endeavored to impose onto reality an illusory utopian vision of humanity, not taking into account the way real people are structured through the force of tradition: on the contrary, Real Socialism failed because it was – in its Stalinist version – ALL TOO "REALISTIC," because it underestimated the REAL of the "illusions" which continued to determine human activity ("bourgeois individualism," etc.), and conceived of the "construction of socialism" as a ruthlessly "realistic" mobilization and exploitation of individuals in order to build a new order. One is thus tempted to claim that, while Lenin still remained faithful to the "real of the (Communist) illusion," to its emancipatory utopian potential, Stalin was a simple "realist," engaged in a ruthless power-struggle.

Each of the two parts of Freud's inaugural dream of Irma's injection concludes with a figuration of the Real. In the conclusion of the first part, this is obvious: the look into Irma's throat renders the Real in the guise of the primordial flesh, the palpitation of the life substance as the Thing itself, in its disgusting dimension of a cancerous outgrowth. However, in the second part, the comic symbolic exchange/interplay of the three doctors also ends up with the Real, this time in its opposite aspect – the Real of writing, of the meaningless formula of trimethylamine. The difference hinges on the different starting point: if we end with the Imaginary (the mirror-confrontation of Freud and Irma), we get the Real in its imaginary dimension, as a horrifying primordial image that cancels the imagery itself; if we start with the Symbolic (the exchange of arguments between the three doctors), we get the signifier itself transformed into the Real of a meaningless letter/formula. Needless to add that these two figures are the very two opposite aspects of the Lacanian Real: the abyss of the primordial Life–Thing and the meaningless letter/ formula (as in the Real of modern science). And, perhaps, one should add to them the third Real, the "Real of the illusion," the Real of a pure semblance, of a spectral dimension which shines through our common reality. There are thus THREE modalities of the Real, i.e. the triad IRS reflects itself within the order of the Real, so that we have the "real Real" (the horrifying Thing, the primordial object, like Irma's throat), the "symbolic Real" (the signifier reduced to a senseless formula, like the quantum physics formulae which can no longer be translated back into – or related to – the everyday experience of our life-world), AND the "imaginary Real" (the mysterious *je ne sais quoi*, the unfathomable "something" that introduces a self-division into an ordinary object, so that the sublime dimension shines through it). If, then, as Lacan put it, Gods are of the Real, the Christian Trinity also has to be read through the lenses of this Trinity of the Real: God the Father is the "real Real" of the violent primordial Thing; God the Son is the "imaginary Real" of the pure *Schein*, the "almost nothing" which the sublime shines through his miserable body; the Holy Ghost is the "symbolic Real" of the community of believers.

A homologous reversal is also to be accomplished if we are to conceive properly the paradoxical status of the Real as impossible. The deconstructionist ethical edifice is based on the IMPOSSIBILITY of the act: the act never happens, it is impossible for it to occur, it is always deferred, about to come, there is forever the gap that separates the impossible fullness of the Act from the limited dimension of our contingent pragmatic intervention (say, the unconditional ethical demand of the Other from the pragmatic political intervention with which we answer it). The fantasy of metaphysics is precisely that the impossible Act CAN or COULD happen, that it would have happened if it were not for some contingent empirical obstacle; the task of the deconstructionist analysis is then to demonstrate how what appears (and is misperceived) as a contingent empirical obstacle actually gives body to a proto-transcendental a priori – such apparently contingent obstacles HAVE to occur; the impossibility is structural, not empirical–contingent. Assume that the illusion of anti-Semitism is that social antagonisms are introduced by the Jewish intervention, so that, if we eliminate Jews, the fully realized non-antagonistic harmonious social body will take place; against this misperception, the critical analysis should demonstrate how the anti-Semitic figure of the Jew gives body to the structural impossibility constitutive of the social order.

It seems that Lacan also fits this logic perfectly: does the illusory fullness of the imaginary fantasy not cover up a structural gap, and does psychoanalysis not assert the heroic acceptance of the fundamental gap and/or structural impossibility as the very condition of desire? Is this, exactly, not the "ethics of the Real" – the ethics of accepting the Real of a structural impossibility? However, what Lacan ultimately aims at is precisely the opposite; let's take the case of love. Lovers usually dream that in some mythical Otherness ("another time, another place"), their love would have found its true fulfillment, that it is only the present contingent circumstances which prevent this fulfillment; and is the Lacanian lesson here not that one should accept this obstacle as structurally necessary, that there is NO "other place" of fulfillment, that this Otherness is the very Otherness of the fantasy? No: the "Real as impossible" means here that THE IMPOSSIBLE DOES HAPPEN, that "miracles" like Love (or political revolution: "in some respects, a revolution is a miracle," Lenin said in 1921) DO occur. From "impossible TO happen" we thus pass to "the impossible HAPPENS" – this, and not the structural obstacle forever deferring the final resolution, is the most difficult thing to accept: "We'd forgotten how to be in readiness even for miracles to happen."[28]

The act proper is thus to be opposed to other modalities of the act: the hysterical acting out, the psychotic *passage à l'acte*, the symbolic act. In the hysterical acting out, the subject stages, in a kind of theatrical performance, the compromise solution of the trauma she is unable to cope with. In the psychotic *passage à l'acte*, the deadlock is so debilitating that the subject cannot even imagine a way out – the only thing he can do is to strike blindly in the real, to release his frustration in the meaningless outburst of destructive energy. The symbolic act is best conceived of as the purely formal, self-referential, gesture of the self-assertion of one's subjective position. Let us take a situation of the political defeat of some working-class initiative; what one should accomplish at this moment to reassert one's identity is precisely the symbolic act: stage a common event in which some shared ritual (song or what-soever) is performed, an event which contains no positive political program – its message is only the purely performative assertion: "We are still here, faithful to our mission, the space is still open for our activity to come!"

Mark Herman's *Brassed Off* focuses on the relationship between the "real" political struggle (the miners' struggle against the threatening pit closure legitimized in terms of technological progress) and the idealized symbolic expression of the miners' community, their playing in the brass band. At first, the two aspects seem to be opposed: to the miners caught in the struggle for their economic survival, the "Only music matters!" attitude of their old band leader dying of lung cancer appears as a vain fetishized insistence of the empty symbolic form deprived of its social substance. However, once the miners lose their political struggle, the "music matters" attitude, their insistence to go on playing and participating in the national competition, turns into a defying symbolic gesture, a proper act of asserting fidelity to their political struggle – as one of the miners puts it, when there is no hope, there are just principles to follow . . . In short, the symbolic act occurs when we arrive at this crossroads, or, rather, short-circuiting of the two levels, so that insistence on the empty form itself ("we'll continue playing in our brass band, whatever happens . . .") becomes the sign of fidelity to the content (to the struggle against the closures, for the continuation of the miners' way of life). In contrast to all these three modes, the act proper is the only one which restructures the very symbolic coordinates of the agent's situation: it is an intervention in the course of which the agent's identity itself is radically changed.

And it's exactly the same with belief: the lesson of Graham

Greene's novels is that religious belief, far from being the pacifying consolation, is the most traumatic thing to accept. Therein resides the ultimate failure of Neil Jordan's *The End of the Affair*, which accomplishes two changes with regard to Greene's novel upon which it is based: it *displaces* the ugly birthmark (and its miraculous disappearance after a kiss by Sarah) from the atheist preacher to the private investigator's son, and it *condenses* two persons (the atheist preacher whom Sarah visited after her shocking encounter with the miracle, i.e. the success of her wager after she finds her lover dead, and the older Catholic priest who tries to console Maurice, the narrator, and Sarah's husband after her death) into one, the preacher whom Sarah is secretly visiting and who is mistaken by Maurice for her lover.[29] This replacement of the agnostic preacher by a priest thoroughly misses the point of Sarah's visits: in a dialectic of faith that is Greene's trademark, she starts to visit him precisely because of his ferocious anti-theism: she wants desperately to ESCAPE her faith, the miraculous proof of God's existence, so she takes refuge with the avowed atheist – with the predictable result that not only does he fail in delivering her of her faith, but that, at the novel's end, he himself becomes a believer (THIS is also the reason why the miracle of the disappearing birthmark has to take place on HIS face!). The psychoanalytic name for such a "miracle," for an intrusion which momentarily suspends the causal network of our daily lives, is, of course, *trauma*. In his *Zollikoner Seminare*, edited by Medard Boss, Heidegger dismisses Freud as a causal determinist:

> He postulates for the conscious human phenomena that they can be explained without gaps, i.e. the continuity of causal connections. Since there are no such connections "in the

consciousness," he has to invent "the unconscious," in which
there have to be the causal links without gaps."[30]

Here, of course, Heidegger completely misses the way the
Freudian "unconscious" is grounded in the traumatic
encounter of an Otherness whose intrusion precisely *breaks*,
interrupts, the continuity of the causal link: what we get in
the "unconscious" is not a complete, uninterrupted, causal
link, but the repercussions, the after-shocks, of traumatic
interruptions.[31] Although there is a similarity between this
Lacanian Real and the notion of the "priority of the objective"
elaborated by Adorno, Heidegger's most embittered critic, it
is this very similarity that renders all the more palpable the
gap that separates them. Adorno's basic endeavor is to reconcile the materialist "priority of the objective" with the idealist
legacy of the subjective "mediation" of all objective reality:
everything we experience as directly-immediately given is
already mediated, posited through a network of differences;
every theory that asserts our access to immediate reality, be it
the phenomenological *Wesensschau* (intuition of the essence)
or the empiricist perception of elementary sensual data, is
false. On the other hand, Adorno also rejects the idealist
notion that all objective content is posited/produced by the
subject – such a stance also fetishizes subjectivity itself into a
given immediacy. This is the reason why Adorno opposes the
Kantian a priori of the transcendental categories which
mediate our access to reality (and thus constitute what we
experience *as* reality): for Adorno, the Kantian transcendental
a priori does not simply absolutize the subjective mediation –
it obliterates *its own* historical mediation. The table of Kantian
transcendental categories is not a pre-historical "pure" a
priori, but a historically "mediated" conceptual network,

i.e., a network embedded in and engendered by a determinate historical constellation. How, then, are we to think TOGETHER the radical mediation of all objectivity and the materialist "priority of the objective"? The solution is that this "priority" is the very result of mediation brought to its end, the kernel of resistance that we cannot experience directly, but only in the guise of the absent point of reference on account of which every mediation ultimately FAILS.

It is a standard argument against Adorno's "negative dialectics" to reproach it for its inherent inconsistency; Adorno's answer is appropriate: stated as a definitive doctrine, as a result, "negative dialectics" effectively IS "inconsistent" – the way to grasp it correctly is to conceive of it as the description of a process of thought (in Lacanese, to include the position of enunciation involved in it). "Negative dialectics" designates a position which includes its own failure, i.e. which produces the truth-effect through its very failure. To put it succinctly: one tries to grasp/conceive the object of thought; one fails, missing it, and through these very failures the place of the targeted object is encircled, its contours become discernible. So what one is tempted to do here is to introduce the Lacanian notion of the "barred" subject ($) and the object as real/impossible: the Adornian distinction between immediately accessible "positive" objectivity and the objectivity targeted in the "priority of the objective" is the very Lacanian distinction between (symbolically mediated) reality and the impossible Real. Furthermore, does the Adornian notion that the subject retains its subjectivity only insofar it is "incompletely" subject, insofar as some kernel of objectivity resists its grasp, not point towards the subject as constitutively "barred"?

There are two ways out of the deadlock in which Adorno's

"negative dialectics" ends, the Habermasian and the Lacanian. Habermas, who perceived Adorno's inconsistency, his self-destructive critique of Reason which cannot account for itself, proposed as a solution the pragmatic a priori of the communicative normativity, a kind of Kantian regulative ideal presupposed in every intersubjective exchange. Lacan, on the contrary, elaborates the *concept* of what Adorno deployed as dialectical paradoxes: the concept of the "barred" subject who exists only through its own impossibility; the concept of the Real as the inherent, not external, limitation of reality.

GOD RESIDES IN DETAILS

At the level of theology, this shift from external to inherent limitation is accomplished by Christianity. In Judaism, God remains the transcendent irrepresentable Other, i.e., as Hegel was right to emphasize, Judaism is the religion of the Sublime: it tries to render the suprasensible dimension not through the overwhelming excess of the sensible, like the Indian statues with dozens of hands, etc., but in a purely negative way, by renouncing images altogether. Christianity, however, renounces this God of Beyond, this Real behind the curtain of the phenomena; it acknowledges that there is NOTHING beyond the appearance – nothing BUT the imperceptible X that changes Christ, this ordinary man, into God. In the ABSOLUTE identity of man and God, the Divine is the pure *Schein* of another dimension that shines through Christ, this miserable creature. It is only here that the iconoclasm is truly brought to its conclusion: what is effectively "beyond the image" is that X that makes the man Christ God. In this precise sense, Christianity inverses the Jewish sublimation into a radical desublimation: not desublimation in the sense of the simple reduction of God to man, but desublimation in the sense of the descendence of the sublime Beyond to the everyday level. Christ is a "ready-made God" (as Boris Groys put it), he is fully human, inherently indistinguishable from other humans in exactly the same way Judy is indistinguishable from Madeleine in *Vertigo*, or the "true" Erhardt is indistinguishable from his impersonator in *To Be Or Not To Be* – it is only the imperceptible "something," a pure appearance which cannot ever be grounded in a substantial property, that makes him divine. THIS is why Christianity is the religion of love and of comedy: as examples from Lubitsch and Chaplin demonstrate, there is always something comic in this unfathomable difference that undermines the established identity (Judy IS Madeleine, Hynkel IS the Jewish barber). And love is to be opposed here to desire: desire is always caught in the logic of "this is not that," it thrives in the gap that forever separates the *obtained* satisfaction from the *sought-for* satisfaction, while love FULLY ACCEPTS that "this IS that" – that the woman with all her weaknesses and common features IS the Thing I unconditionally love; that Christ, this wretched man, IS the living God. Again, to avoid a fatal misunderstanding: the point is not that we should "renounce transcendence" and fully accept the limited human person as our love object, since "this is all there is": transcendence is not abolished, but rendered ACCESSIBLE[32] – it shines through in this very clumsy and miserable being that I love.

Christ is thus not "man PLUS God": what becomes visible in him is simply the divine dimension in man "as such." So, far from being the Highest in man, the purely spiritual dimension towards which all humans strive, the "divinity" is rather a kind of obstacle, of a "bone in the throat" – it is something, that unfathomable X, on account of which man cannot ever fully become MAN, self-identical. The point is not that, due to the limitation of his mortal sinful nature, man cannot ever become fully divine, but that, due to the divine spark in him, man cannot ever fully become MAN. Christ as man = God is the unique case of full humanity (*ecce homo*, as Pontius Pilatus put it to the mob demanding the lynching of Christ). For that reason, after his death, there is no place for any God of Beyond: all that remains is the Holy Spirit, the community of believers onto which the unfathomable aura of Christ passes once it is deprived of its bodily incarnation (or, to put it in Freudian terms, once it can no longer rely on the *Anlehnung* (the notion of leaning on Christ's body), in the same sense as, for Freud, the drive which aims at unconditional satisfaction, always has to "lean on" a particular, contingent material object which acts as the source of its satisfaction).

This reading has radical consequences for the notion of an afterlife. The often noted enigmatic lapse in Judaism concerns afterlife: its sacred texts NEVER mention the afterlife – it is a religion which seems to renounce the very basic feature of what religion is supposed to do, i.e. bring us consolation by promising us a happy afterlife. And it is crucial to reject as secondary falsification any notion that Christianity DOES return to the tradition of an afterlife (individuals will be judged by God, and then enter either Hell or Paradise). As it was already noted by, among others, Kant, such a notion of Christianity which involves the just payment for our deeds reduces it to just another religion of moral accountancy, of the just reward or punishment for our deeds. If one conceives of the Holy Spirit in the consequent way, there is simply NO PLACE in the Christian edifice for an afterlife.

In other words, tragedy and comedy are also to be opposed along the axis of the opposition between desire and drive. As

Lacan emphasized throughout his teaching, not only is desire inherently "tragic" (condemned to its ultimate failure), tragedy itself (in all the classic cases, from Oedipus and Antigone through Hamlet up to Claudel's Coufontaine trilogy) is ultimately always the tragedy of desire. Drive, on the contrary, is inherently COMIC in its "closing the loop" and suspending the gap of desire, in its assertion of the coincidence, identity even, between the sublime and the everyday object. Of course, the gap persists in drive, in the guise of the distance between its aim – satisfaction – and its goal – the object on which it "leans" (it is because of this gap that drive is forever condemned to a circular movement); however, this gap, instead of opening up the infinite metonymy of desire, sustains the closed loop (or warp) of the drive. In Kafka's "A Fasting Showman", towards the end of the endless process of fasting, the dying showman reveals his secret:

> " . . . I have to fast, I can't do anything else," said the fasting showman.
>
> "What a fellow you are," said the overseer, "and why can't you do anything else?" "Because," said the fasting showman, lifting his head a little and speaking with his lips pursed, as if for a kiss, right into the overseer's ear, so that no syllable might be lost, "because I couldn't find any food I liked. If I had found any, believe me, I should have made no bones about it and stuffed myself like you or anyone else."
>
> These were his last words . . . [33]

What strikes the eye here is the contrast with Kafka's most famous text, "Before the Law" from *The Trial*, in which, towards the end of the life-long waiting in front of the Door of the Law, the gatekeeper also whispers into the ears of the dying man from the country the secret of the Doors (they were made only for him, no one else could have been admitted there, so after his death, they will be closed): in "A Fasting Showman," it is the dying man himself who reveals his secret to his keeper–overseer, while in *The Trial*, it is the keeper–overseer who reveals the secret to the dying man. Where does this opposition come from, if, in both cases, the secret revealed at the end concerns a certain Void (the lack of proper food, there is nothing beyond the door)? The fasting showman stands for drive at its purest: he gives body to the Lacanian distinction between "not eating" and "eating the Nothing", i.e. by fasting, by rejecting every offered object-food because *ce n'est pas ça*, he eats Nothing itself, the void which sets in motion desire – he repeatedly circulates around the central void. The man from the country, on the contrary, is a hysteric whose desire is obsessed by the Secret (the Thing) Beyond the Door. So, contrary to the misleading first impression, Kafka's fasting showman is NOT an anorexic: anorexia is one of today's forms of hysteria (the classic Freudian hysteria reacts to the traditional figure of the patriarchal master, while anorexia reacts to the reign of expert knowledge).

The key distinction to be maintained here can be exemplified by the (apparent) opposite of religion, the intense sexual experience. Eroticization relies on the inversion-into-self of the movement directed at an external goal: the movement itself becomes its own goal. (When, instead of simply gently shaking the hand offered to me by the beloved person, I hold it and repeatedly squeeze it, my activity will be automatically experienced as – welcome or, perhaps, intrusively unwelcome – eroticization: what I do is change the goal-oriented activity into an end-in-itself.) Therein resides the difference between the goal and the aim of a drive: say, with regard to the oral drive, its goal may be to eliminate hunger, but its aim is the satisfaction provided by the activity of eating (sucking, swallowing) itself. One can imagine the two satisfactions entirely separated: when, in a hospital, I am fed intravenously, my hunger is satisfied, but not my oral drive; when, on the contrary, a small child rhythmically sucks the comforter, the only satisfaction he gets is that of the drive. This gap that separates aim from goal "eternalizes" drive, transforming the simple instinctual movement which finds peace and calm when it reaches its goal (say, the full stomach) into the process which gets caught in its own loop and insists on endlessly repeating itself. The crucial feature to take note of here is that this inversion cannot be formulated in terms of the primordial lack and the series of metonymic objects trying (and, ultimately, failing) to fill in its void. When the eroticized body of my partner starts to function as the object around which drive circulates, this does NOT mean that his/her ordinary ("pathological," in the Kantian sense of the term) flesh-and-blood body is "transubstantiated" into a contingent embodiment of the sublime impossible Thing, holding (filling out) its empty place.

Let us take a direct "vulgar" example: when a (heterosexual male) lover is fascinated with his partner's vagina, "never getting enough of it," prone not only to penetrate it, but to explore it and caress it in all possible ways, the point is NOT that, in a kind of deceptive short-circuit, he mistakes the piece of skin, hair and flesh for the Thing itself – his lover's vagina is, in all its bodily materiality, "the thing itself," not the spectral appearing of another dimension; what makes it an "infinitely" desirable object whose "mystery" cannot ever be fully penetrated, is its non-identity to itself, i.e. the way it is never directly "itself."[34] The gap which "eternalizes" drive, turning it into the endlessly repetitive circular movement around the object, is not the gap that separates the void of the Thing from its contingent embodiments, but the gap that separates the very "pathological" object FROM ITSELF, in the same way that, as we have just seen, Christ is not the contingent material ("pathological") embodiment of the suprasensible God: his "divine" dimension is reduced to the aura of a pure *Schein*.

Therein resides the problem with Bernard Baas's outstanding Kantian reading of Lacan in his *De la Chose à l'objet*,[35] this heroic endeavor to think together the Kantian "transcendental" reading of Lacan with the problematic of the *presubjective* drive, of that obscure process in the course of which a living body "explodes" into a self-sentient organism which is at the same time inside and outside itself (it is part of the objective environs in which it exists as an object, while, at the same time, it contains the world in its field of vision). We are thus dealing with what Lacan refers to as the mysterious "doubling *(la doublure)*"[36] of the living body: a gap, distance, is introduced, a gap which involves the paradoxical topology of the Möbius strip or Klein's bottle.[37] It is in this "doubling" which is not yet the subjective redoubling characteristic of self-reflexion and/or self-consciousness, that Lacan discerns the fundamental structure of the "acephalous" drive whose best metaphor is a pair of lips kissing themselves. The mysterious intermediate status of drive resides in the fact that, while we are NOT YET dealing with the subject submitted to the symbolic Law, condemned to the eternal search for the primordial lost object ("Thing") which is already missing in reality, we are also NO LONGER dealing with the immediate self-enclosure of a biological organism: from the standpoint of "mere (biological) life," a certain *excess* is already at work here, a certain "too much," the addiction to a surplus which can no longer be contained – what is "drive" if not the name for an excessive "pressure" which derails/disturbs the purely biological life-rhythm.

Eric Santner connects this excess to the old Heraclitian formula *hen diapheron heauto*, to which Plato refers in his *Symposium*, and which Hölderlin, in his *Hyperion*, translates as "das Eine in sich selber unterschiedene" – the one differentiated in itself.[38] And, as Santner points out, when Hölderlin endorses this formula as the very definition of beauty, the point is not that artists reconcile the opposites and tensions in the aesthetic Totality of a harmonious Whole, but, on the contrary, that they construct a place in which people can ecstatically perceive the traumatic excess around which their life turns. Along these lines, Santner proposes a new reading of Hölderlin's famous lines from his hymn *Andenken*: "Was bleibet aber, stiften die Dichter" ("But poets establish what remains"). The standard reading, of course, is that, after the event, poets are able to perceive the situation from the mature standpoint after the fact, i.e. from the safe distance when the historical meaning of the events become clear. What if, however, what remains is *the remainder itself*, what Schelling called the "indivisible remainder," that which STICKS OUT from the organic Whole, the excess which cannot be incorporated/ integrated into the socio-historical Totality, so that, far from providing the harmonious total image of an epoch, poetry gives voice to that which an epoch was UNABLE to include in its narrative(s)? The fact that the original formula (*hen diapheron heauto*) is Heraclitian should make us attentive: one should read it "anachronistically," against the grain, i.e. NOT in its original pre-Socratic sense of the harmony of the All which emerges from the very struggle and tension of its parts, but as focused on that excess which prevents the One from ever turning into a harmonious All. It is as if Heraclitus's words are to be conceived of as a fragment pointing towards the future, coming from the future: only an "anachronistic" reading from the future can discern its true meaning.

How, then, can Baas bring together this notion of drive and his earlier brilliant Kantian reading of Lacan which emphasizes the structural homology between the Freudian–Lacanian Thing and the Kantian noumenal Thing-in-itself: the Thing is nothing but its own lack, the elusive specter of the lost primordial object of desire engendered by the symbolic Law/Prohibition, and *l'objet petit a* is the Lacanian "transcendental scheme" which mediates between the a priori void of the impossible Thing and the empirical objects that give us (dis)pleasure – *objets a* are empirical objects contingently elevated to the dignity of the Thing, so that they start to function as embodiments of the impossible Thing?[39] Baas's solution is predictable: in its self-enclosed circulation, drive achieves its aim by repeatedly missing its goal, which means that it rotates around a central Void, and this Void is the Void of/as the impossible/real Thing, prohibited/lost once the subject emerges through entering the symbolic order ... At this point, however, one should insist that the "doubling," the topological torsion which brings about the "excess" of life we call "drive," CANNOT be equated to (or grounded in) the symbolic Law which prohibits the impossible maternal Real Thing: the gap opened up by this "doubling" is NOT the void of the Thing prohibited by the symbolic Law. One is almost tempted to say that the ultimate function of the symbolic Law is to enable us to AVOID the debilitating deadlock of drive – the symbolic Law already reacts to a certain inherent impediment on account of which the animal instinct somehow gets "stuck" and explodes in the excessive repetitive movement, it enables the subject to magically transform this repetitive movement through which the subject is stuck with and for the drive's cause–object, into the eternal open search for the (lost/prohibited) object of desire. To put it in a slightly different way: while Baas is right to insist that the "doubling" of the drive always occurs within the order of the signifier, he equates *signifier* with *the symbolic order* grounded in the Law/ Prohibition too readily: what Lacan was endeavoring to elaborate in the last two decades of his teaching was precisely the status of *a signifier not yet contained within the symbolic Law/Prohibition*. Nowhere is this distinction clearer than apropos of sublimation (if we follow Lacan in defining it as the elevation of an (empirical) object to the dignity of the Thing[40]): the drive does NOT "elevate an (empirical) object to the dignity of the Thing" – it rather chooses as its object an object which has in itself the circular structure of rotating around a void.

We all know the phrase "the devil resides in the details" – implying that, in an agreement, you should be attentive to the proverbial small-print specifications and conditions at the bottom of the page which may contain unpleasant surprises, and, for all practical purposes, nullify what the agreement offers. Does this phrase hold also for theology? Is it really that God is discernible in the overall harmony of the universe, while the Devil sticks in small features which, while insignificant from the global perspective, can mean terrible suffering for us, individuals? With regard to Christianity, at least, one is tempted to turn around this formula: *God resides in details* – in the overall drabness and indifference of the universe, we discern the divine dimension in barely perceptible details – a kind smile here, an unexpected helpful gesture there . . . The Turin Shroud with the alleged photographic imprint of Christ is perhaps the ultimate case of this "divine detail," of the "little bit of the real" – the debates about it neatly fall into the triad IRS: the Imaginary (is the image discernible on it the faithful reproduction of Christ?), the Real (when was the material made? Is the test which demonstrated that the linen was woven in the fourteenth century conclusive?), the Symbolic (the narrative of the Shroud's complicated destiny through the centuries). The true problem, however, resides in the potentially catastrophic consequences for the Church itself if the tests indicate again that the Shroud is authentic (from Christ's time and place): there are traces of "Christ"'s blood on it, and some biochemists are already working on its DNA – so what will this DNA say about Christ's FATHER (not to mention the prospect of CLONING Christ)?

Does this minimal self-distance of a living being into which this excess inscribes itself, this gap or redoubling of life into "ordinary" life and the spectral "undead" life, not display the structure of what Marx described as the "commodity fetishism" – an ordinary object acquires the aura, another incorporeal dimension starts to shine through it? As Lacan himself emphasized,[41] the answer is that commodity fetishism itself parasitizes upon the structure of "immanent transcendence" which pertains to drive as such: in certain social conditions, the products of human labor mobilize this function, appearing as the universe of commodities. With regard to the figure of Christ, this reference to the universe of commodities also enables us to reactualize Marx's old idea that Christ is like money among men – ordinary commodities: in the same way money as universal equivalent directly embodies/assumes the excess ("Value") that makes an object a commodity, Christ directly embodies/assumes the excess that makes the human animal a proper human being. In both cases, then, the universal equivalent exchanges/gives itself for all other excesses – in the same way money is the commodity "as such," Christ is man "as such"; in the same way that the universal equivalent has to be a commodity deprived of any use value, Christ has taken over the excess of Sin of ALL men precisely insofar as he was the Pure one, without excess, simplicity itself.

In order to elucidate the elementary structure of this excess, let us turn to Jonathan Lear, who deploys a powerful critique of the Freudian "death drive": Freud hypostasizes into a positive teleological principle the purely negative fact of breaks and interruptions which cannot be directly contained/integrated in the "normal" teleologically oriented psychic economy; instead of accepting the fact of purely contingent interruptions which undermine the teleological functioning of the human psyche, he fantasizes a higher positive tendency/principle that accounts for these disruptions ("death drive").[42] Lear accuses Lacan of the same reifying positivization of the gap/break into a positive "Beyond" apropos of the notion of the Thing as the Beyond, the unattainable hard kernel of the Real around which signifiers circulate. Instead of accepting that there is always some rest which cannot be accounted for in the terms of the "principle(s)" governing psychic life, Freud invents a higher principle that should effectively encompass the entire psychic life. In a nicely elaborated parallel between Aristotle and Freud, and borrowing the term from Laplanche, Lear specifies this operation as that of introducing the "enigmatic signifier": Freud's "death drive" is not a positive concept with a specific content, but a mere promise of some unspecified knowledge, the designation of a seductive mystery, of an entity which seems to account for the phenomena to be explained, although no one knows exactly what it means.

Is Lacan effectively guilty here? Is it not that the operation of the "enigmatic signifier" as described by Lear is the very operation of the Master-Signifier, of the universality and its constitutive exception? Lacan is not only aware of the trap of "substantializing" the rupture into a Beyond – he elaborated the "feminine" logic of the Non-All precisely in order to counter this logic of the universality and its exception. To put it succinctly, what Lear calls "break" is the space of what Lacan calls the *act*, the rupture in the symbolic narrative continuum, the "possibility of new possibilities," as Lear puts it, and the elementary "masculine" operation is precisely that of obliterating this dimension of the act. Crucial here is Lear's delineation of Freud's break with Aristotelian ethics. Aristotle posits happiness as the goal of life – however, this is already a REFLECTED attitude (following Socrates), since in a pre-philosophical immersion into one's life-world, the question about the meaning and/or the goal of life "as such," in its entirety, cannot emerge. Which means that, in order to answer this question, to deal with life as a Whole, one has to introduce an exception, an element which no longer fits "normal" life (in Aristotle, this, of course, is pure Theory as the supreme self-satisfying activity), which, however, is ultimately inaccessible to us, mortals, since only God(s) can practice it. At the very moment when the philosopher merely tries to conceive what would it mean to live a happy life, he thereby generates a foreign excess on account of which life can no longer be contained in itself ... What Lear (re)discovers here in his own terms is Lacan's paradoxical logic of Non-All: every totalization has to rely on an empty Master-Signifier which marks its constitutive exception. Consequently, does not Lacan's logic of Non-All provide the very formula of what Lear calls "living with a remainder," abandoning the effort to contain the remainder by attaching it to a Master-Signifier and thus "resubstantializing" it, accepting that we dwell within a field that cannot ever be totalized?

Life thus loses its tautological self-satisfactory evidence: it comprises an excess which disturbs its balanced run. What does this mean? The premise of the theory of risk society and global reflexivization is that, today, one can be "addicted" to anything – not only to alcohol or drugs, but also to food, smoking, sex, work ... This universalization of addiction points towards the radical uncertainty of any subjective position today: there are no firm predetermined patterns, everything has to be (re)negotiated again and again, up to and including suicide. Albert Camus, in his otherwise hopelessly outdated The Myth of Sisyphus, is right to emphasize that suicide is the only real philosophical problem – however, WHEN does it become this? Only in the modern reflexive society, when life itself no longer "goes by itself," as a "non-marked" feature (to use the term developed by Roman Jakobson), but is "marked," has to be especially motivated (which is why euthanasia is becoming acceptable). Prior to modernity, suicide was simply a sign of some pathological malfunction, despair, misery. With reflexivization, however, suicide becomes an existential act, the outcome of a pure decision, irreducible to objective suffering or psychic pathology. This is the other side of Emile Durkheim's reduction of suicide to a social fact that can be quantified and predicted: the two moves, the objectivization/quantification of suicide and its transformation into a pure existential act, are strictly correlative. So, in short, what this loss of the spontaneous propensity to live means is that life itself becomes an object of addiction,[43] marked/stained by an excess, containing a "remainder" which no longer fits the simple life process. "To live" no

longer means simply to pursue the balanced process of reproduction, but to get "passionately attached" or stuck to some
excess, to some kernel of the Real, whose role is contradict-
ory: it introduces the aspect of fixity or "fixation" into the life
process – man is ultimately an animal whose life is derailed
through the excessive fixation to some traumatic Thing.

In one of his (unpublished) seminars, Jacques-Alain Miller
comments on an uncanny laboratory experiment with rats: in
a labyrinthine set-up, a desired object (a piece of good food
or a sexual partner) is first made easily accessible to a rat;
then, the set-up is changed in such a way that the rat sees and
thereby knows where the desired object is, but cannot gain
access to it; in exchange for it, as a kind of consolation prize, a
series of similar objects of inferior value is made easily accessible – how does the rat react to it? For some time, it tries to
find its way to the "true" object; then, upon ascertaining that
this object is definitely out of reach, the rat will renounce it
and some of the inferior substitute objects – in short, it will
act as a "rational" subject of utilitarianism. It is only now,
however, that the true experiment begins: the scientists
performed a surgical operation on the rat, messing about with
its brain, doing things to it with laser beams about which, as
Miller put it delicately, it is better to know nothing.

So what happened when the operated rat was again let
loose in the labyrinth, the one in which the "true" object is
inaccessible? *The rat insisted*: it never became fully reconciled
with the loss of the "true" object and resigned itself to one of
the inferior substitutes, but repeatedly returned to the "true"
object and attempted to reach it. In short, the rat in a sense
was *humanized*, it assumed the tragic "human" relationship
towards the unattainable absolute object which, on account of
its very inaccessibility, forever captivates our desire. (Miller's

point, of course, is that this quasi-humanization of the rat resulted from its biological *mutilation*: the unfortunate rat started to act like a human being in relationship to its object of desire when its brain was butchered and crippled by means of an "unnatural" surgical intervention.) On the other hand, it is this very "conservative" fixation that pushes man to continuing renovation, since he never can fully integrate this excess into his life process. So we can see why Freud used the term "death drive": the lesson of psychoanalysis is that humans are not simply alive, but possessed by a strange drive to enjoy life in excess of the ordinary run of things – and "death" stands simply and precisely for the dimension beyond "ordinary" biological life.

Human life is never "just life," it is always sustained by an excess of life which, phenomenally, appears as the paradoxical wound that makes us "undead," which prevents us from dying (apart from Tristan's and Amfortas's in Wagner's *Tristan* and *Parsifal*, the ultimate figure of this wound is found in Kafka's "The Country Doctor"): when this wound is healed, the hero can die in peace. On the other hand, as Jonathan Lear is right to emphasize, the figures of the Ideal Life above the daily routine of life (like the Aristotelian contemplation) are all implicit stand-ins for death: the only way to directly get at the excess of life is, again, to die. The basic Christian insight is to combine these two opposite aspects of the same paradox: getting rid of the wound, healing it, is ultimately the same as fully and directly identifying with it – this is the ambiguity inscribed into the figure of Christ. He stands for the excess of life, for the "undead" surplus which persists over the cycle of generation and corruption: "I am come that they might have life, and that they might have it more abundantly" (*John* 10:10). However, does his sacrifice simultaneously not stand for the obliteration of this excess? The story of the (Adam's) Fall is evidently the story of how the human animal contracted the excess of Life which makes him/her human – "Paradise" is the name for the life delivered of the burden of this disturbing excess. Out of love for humanity, Christ then freely assumes, contracts onto himself, the excess ("Sin") which burdened the human race.

Was Nietzsche right, then, in his claim that Christ was the only true Christian? By taking upon himself all the Sins and then, through his death, paying for them, Christ opens up the way for the redemption of humanity – however, by his death, people are not directly redeemed, but given the POSSIBILITY of redemption, of getting rid of the excess. This distinction is crucial: Christ does NOT do our work for us, he does not pay our debt, he "merely" GIVES US A CHANCE – with his death, he asserts OUR freedom and responsibility, i.e. he "merely" opens up the possibility, for us, to redeem ourselves through the "leap into faith," i.e. by way of choosing to "live in Christ" – in *imitatio Christi*, we REPEAT Christ's gesture of freely assuming the excess of Life, instead of projecting/ displacing it onto some figure of the Other. (We put "merely" in quotation marks, because, as was clear to Kierkegaard, the definition of freedom is that possibility is higher than actuality: by giving us a chance to redeem ourselves, Christ does infinitely more than if he were directly to redeem ourselves.)

"Father, Why Did You Forsake Me?"
Three

One can conceive each big break in the history of the West as a kind of "unplugging": the Greek philosophical wondering "unplugs" from the immersion into the mythical universe; Judaism "unplugs" from the polytheistic *jouissance*; Christianity "unplugs" from one's substantial community. The big question here is: how are these three unpluggings interrelated? Its consequences reverberate in the details of the history of philosophy – recall the total absence of the reference to Judaism as distinct from Christianity and, more specifically, to Spinoza in Heidegger's opus.[1] Why this absence? Perhaps the key is provided by the passage from Heidegger I (*Sein und Zeit* [Being and Time]) to Heidegger II (the epochal historicity of Being). Let us begin with *Sein und Zeit*: the book's second part in a way REPEATS the first part, accomplishing again the analysis of *Dasein* at a more radical level. No wonder Hubert Dreyfus, Richard Rorty, and other partisans of the "pragmatist" reading of Heidegger emphasize the first part: focuses on "being-in-the-world," on *Dasein*'s immersion in its life-world, where it encounters things as "ready-at-hand," and then deploys other modes of relating to things as arising from deficiencies in our immersion in the life-world: when a tool doesn't function properly, we adopt a distance and ask ourselves what is wrong, treating it as a present object. In the second part, however, the perspective is as it were reversed: the immersion in the life-world itself is not the original fact, but is conceived of as secondary with regard to the abyss of *Dasein*'s "thrown-ness," the state of being-thrown into the world, which is experienced in the mode of anxiety disclosing to *Dasein* its constitutive nullity and guilt/responsibility – it is ultimately from this abyss that we escape into engaged immersion in the world, where there is always "something to do."

This repetition, however, is not the whole story – it is supplemented by the last pages of *Sein und Zeit* in which, again, Heidegger moves to a different level, endeavoring to elaborate the passage from *Dasein*'s historicity to the collective history of a people, dealing with notions like the choice of a hero and the *people's* (not individual's) assuming its destiny through the act of decisive opening. The problem with *Sein und Zeit* is not that the book is unfinished, but that it is TOO LONG, containing an excess which is superfluous, not fitting the rest of the book – Heidegger's problem after *Sein und Zeit* was not how to finish the book, but how to get rid of – how to accommodate, find a proper place for – the excess at its end. In the late 1920s, he was desperately looking for a way within what, ultimately, one cannot but designate as the Kantian transcendental horizon, for some time playing with the idea of referring to Kant's transcendental schematism or the moral Law as the background for the proper understanding of *Sein und Zeit*.[2] It is our contention that, if Heidegger were to persevere on this path and pursue it to its end, he would open up, in his theoretical edifice, the place for the fundamental Judeo-Christian experience of the human essence grounded in a traumatic encounter of a radical Otherness, and of this divine Otherness itself needing man, humanity, as the place of its revelation. It was in a gesture of DEFEAT that, in the mid-1930s, Heidegger opted for what many critics, including Philippe Lacoue-Labarthe,[3] denounced as his aesthetico-political notion of the community (*polis* as the place of communal dwelling). Strictly correlative to this aestheticization of politics is Heidegger's reinscription of the abyssal excess of history into the notion of the heroic act: excess is ultimately the excessive-monstrous gesture of a hero who grounds a new *polis* . . . This, then, also provides an answer to why the reference to the Jewish experience is totally absent from Heidegger's thought: the place for it is IN BETWEEN Heidegger I and Heidegger II, i.e. it would have opened itself up if Heidegger had gone to the end on the "transcendental" path of *Sein und Zeit*.

In his well-known determination of the beginnings of Western philosophy, Heidegger celebrates Socrates as the "purest thinker of the West," which is why "he wrote nothing." With regard to the "draft" of the withdrawal of Being which attracts us by its withdrawal, he "did nothing else than place himself into this draft, this current, and maintain himself in it," so that all great philosophers after Socrates are ultimately fugitives, they behave "like those people who run to seek refuge from any draft too strong for them."[4] In Lacanian terms, this "draft" of the withdrawal is the gap in the big Other, so that Socrates was the only one who endured in this gap, who acted as a stand-in and place-holder, who, for his interlocutors, gave body, occupied the space of this gap. All subsequent philosophers concealed this gap by providing a closed ontological edifice. Was Lacan not right when, in his seminar on Transference, he conceived of the position of Socrates as that of the analyst who also occupies the place of *objet petit a*, of the lack/inconsistency of the big Other?[5] Does Socrates not stand for the ex-timate kernel of philosophy, for the non-philosophical position of the analyst which gives birth to philosophy, although it is necessarily obfuscated by its development? It is crucial here that Heidegger defines Socrates in purely structural terms: what matters is the structural place (of the inconsistency of the Other) he occupies, in which he persists, not the positive content of his teaching. So when Heidegger emphasizes that Socrates "wrote nothing," the accent is here not on writing as opposed to pure speech, but on the absence of "works," of the systematic exposition of a teaching – "Socrates" names just a certain POSITION of enunciation, that of "unplugging" from the community, for which he paid with his life, not a set of propositions.

FAITH WITHOUT BELIEF

Let us, then, begin with the Jewish break. First and foremost, it concerns the changed status of faith. In his "Je sais bien, mais quand même . . . ,"[6] Octave Mannoni develops the difference between "faith (foi)" and "belief (croyance)": when I say "I have faith in you," I assert the symbolic pact between the two of us, a binding engagement, the dimension which is absent in simple "believing in . . ." (spirits, etc.). Apropos of the ancient Jews, they BELIEVED IN many gods and spirits, but what Jehovah demanded from them was to HAVE FAITH only in Him, to respect the symbolic pact between the Jewish people and their God who has chosen them. One can believe in ghosts without having faith in them, i.e. without believing them (considering them tricky and evil, not feeling bound to them by any pact or commitment); and, in a more tricky but crucial opposite case, one can believe (have faith in) X without believing in X. The later, for Lacan, is the very case of the big Other, the symbolic Order: "there is no big Other," it is just a virtual order, a shared fiction, we do not have to believe IN

IT in order to believe IT, to feel bound by some symbolic commitment. For that very reason, in the case of the imaginary "belief in," belief is always displaced (it is never me who, in the first person singular, is ready to assume belief, there is always the need for the fiction of a "subject supposed to belief"), while in the case of the symbolic faith, the commitment in the first person singular is performatively assumed.

However, is it not that ALL religion, ALL experience of the sacred, involves – or, rather, simply IS – an "unplugging" from the daily routine? Is this "unplugging" not simply the name for the basic ECSTATIC experience of entering the domain in which everyday rules are suspended, the domain of the sacred TRANSGRESSION? For the Jews, on the contrary, the Law itself unplugs us from daily rules/regulations – in and through the "unplugging," we do not engage in the orgies that suspend the Law, we encounter *the Law itself* as the most radical transgression. One should recall here again, from Kafka's *The Trial*, the discussion between Josef K. and the priest after (and about) the parable of the Door of the Law: what cannot but strike the eye is the totally non-initiatic, non-mystical, purely "external," pedantically-legal nature of this discussion. In these unsurpassable pages, Kafka practices the unique Jewish art of reading as the manipulation of the signifier, of the "dead letter," best rendered by the commentators' motto quoted by the priest: "The right perception of any matter and a misunderstanding of the same matter do not wholly exclude each other."[7] Suffice it to mention the priest's claim that the really deluded person in the parable is not the man from the country, but the door-keeper himself who "is subject to the man and does not know it"[8] – why? A bondman is always subject to a free man, and it is obviously the man from the country who is free: he can go where he likes, he came to the Door of the Law out of his own free will, while the door-keeper is bound to his post. Since the door was meant only for the man from the country, the door-keeper had to be waiting there for years for the man from the country's whimsical decision to go to the Door of the Law . . .'[9] – can one imagine a starker contrast to the ecstatic obscurantist hermeneutics looking for secret spiritual messages? There is no mystical Secret that we are approaching here, no Grail to be uncovered, just dry bureaucratic haggling – which, of course, makes the whole procedure all the more uncanny and enigmatic.[10]

Does Judaism effectively open up the dimension "beyond history?" Yes and no: it is only with Judeo-Christian tradition that history proper BEGINS – history as opposed to simple organic development or the cycle of generation and corruption of empires. History proper IS the tension between history and the "eternal" (ahistorical) traumatic kernel. Here, one is even tempted to praise the unfortunate half-forgotten Francis Fukuyama: the idea of the "end of history" is much closer to the true historical approach than the simplistic globalized historicism (i.e. the naive counter-argument that history is far from over, that struggles and changes continue), since it involves the notion of a radical BREAK, the rupture between BEFORE and AFTER – and such a rupture in the continuum of evolution IS the mark of HISTORY – "history" in the radical sense of the term is nothing but the succession of such ruptures which redefine the very MEANING of history. Therein resides the ultimate paradox: it is the advocates of the "end of history" who, on account of their notion of a radical rupture between BEFORE and AFTER, between history and post-history, are much closer to true historicity than those who mock them, insisting that history goes on, that the struggles are far from over – these "struggles" are flat, a mere process of generation and corruption, a "natural history" lacking the proper historical tension.

And, incidentally, therein also resides the fatal limitation of the standard historicist criticism of Alain Badiou's work, according to which, the intervention *ex nihilo* of the Event into the historicity of Being is a laicized version of the religious Revelation through which Eternity directly intervenes in the temporal unfolding: is it not that Badiou himself emphasizes how one cannot derive the Event from the order of Being, since all we have in the order of Being is *la site événèmentielle*, the site of the potential emergence of the Event of Truth?[11] The first problem with this reproach is that it knocks on an open door: Badiou himself repeatedly refers to the Event as the laicized Grace.[12] More fundamentally, what these reproaches fail to see is, again, the gap that forever separates history (in the sense of a simple dynamic evolutionary unfolding) from historicity proper whose site is none other than the very tension between Eternity and History, the unique moments of their short-circuiting. Which is why, against occasional misleading formulations by Badiou himself, one should assert that there is no ultimate "synthesis" between Event and Being: *this "synthesis" is already the Event itself*, the "magic" appearance of the "noumenal" dimension of Truth in the order of Being. No wonder, then, that in his notion of the Event of Truth as external and irreducible to the process of Being, Badiou gets involved with some strange bedfellows whom he otherwise violently disavows. In her "What is Freedom?," Hannah Arendt asserts that, far from being controllable and predictable, an act of freedom is closer to the nature of a miracle: freedom is displayed in a capacity "to begin something new and . . . not being able to control or even foretell its consequences."[13] A free act thus involves:

> [the] *abyss* of nothingness that opens up before any deed that cannot be accounted for by a reliable chain of cause and effect and is inexplicable in Aristotelian categories of potentiality and actuality.[14]

For Arendt, and in a strict homology to Badiou, freedom is thus opposed to the whole domain of the provision of services and goods, of the maintenance of households and the exercise of administration, which do not belong to politics proper: the only place for freedom is the communal political space. What thereby gets lost is no less than Marx's fundamental insight into how "the problem of freedom is contained in the social relations implicitly declared 'unpolitical' – that is, naturalized – in liberal discourse."[15]

THE LENINIST FREEDOM

How, then, do things stand with freedom? Here is how Lenin stated his position in a polemic against the Menshevik and Socialist-Revolutionaries' critique of Bolshevik power in 1922:

> Indeed, the sermons which . . . the Mensheviks and Socialist-Revolutionaries preach express their true nature: "The revolution has gone too far. What you are saying now we have been saying all the time, permit us to say it again." But we say in reply: "Permit us to put you before a firing squad for saying that. Either you refrain from expressing your views, or, if you insist on expressing your political views publicly in the present circumstances, when our position is far more difficult than it was when the white guards were directly attacking us,

> then you will have only yourselves to blame if we treat you as
> the worst and most pernicious white guard elements."[16]

This Leninist freedom of choice − not "Life or money!" but "Life or critique!" − combined with Lenin's dismissive attitude towards the "liberal" notion of freedom, accounts for his bad reputation among liberals. Their case largely rests upon their rejection of the standard Marxist–Leninist opposition of "formal" and "actual" freedom: as even Leftist liberals like Claude Lefort emphasize again and again, freedom is in its very notion "formal," so that "actual freedom" equals the lack of freedom.[17] That is to say, with regard to freedom, Lenin is best remembered for his famous retort "Freedom − yes, but for WHOM? To do WHAT?" − for him, in the case of the Mensheviks quoted above, their "freedom" to criticize the Bolshevik government effectively amounted to "freedom" to undermine the workers' and peasants' government on behalf of the counterrevolution . . . Today, is it not obvious after the terrifying experience of Really Existing Socialism, where the fault of this reasoning resides? First, it reduces a historical constellation to a closed, fully contextualized, situation in which the "objective" consequences of one's acts are fully determined ("independently of your intentions, what you are doing now objectively serves . . . "); second, the position of enunciation of such statements usurps the right to decide what your acts "objectively mean," so that their apparent "objectivism" (the focus on "objective meaning") is the form of appearance of its opposite, the thorough *subjectivism*: I decide what your acts objectively mean, since I define the context of a situation (say, if I conceive of my power as the immediate equivalent/expression of the power of the working class, then everyone who opposes me is "objectively" an

On Belief

enemy of the working class). Against this full contextualiza-
tion, one should emphasize that freedom is "actual" precisely
and only as the capacity to "transcend" the coordinates of a
given situation, to "posit the presuppositions" of one's activity (as Hegel would have put it), i.e. to redefine the very
situation within which one is active. Furthermore, as many a
critic pointed out, the very term "Really Existing Socialism,"
although it was coined in order to assert Socialism's success,
is in itself a proof of Socialism's utter failure, i.e. of the failure
of the attempt to legitimize Socialist regimes – the term
"Really Existing Socialism" popped up at the historical
moment when the only legitimizing reason for Socialism was
a mere fact that it exists . . . [18]

Is this, however, the whole story? How does freedom
effectively function in liberal democracies themselves?
Although Clinton's presidency epitomizes the Third Way of
today's (ex-)Left succumbing to the Rightist ideological
blackmail, his healthcare reform program would nonetheless
amount to a kind of *act*, at least in today's conditions, since it
would have been based on the rejection of the hegemonic
notions of the need to curtail Big State expenditure and
administration – in a way, it would "do the impossible." No
wonder, then, that it failed: its failure – perhaps the only
significant, although negative, *event* of Clinton's presidency –
bears witness to the material force of the ideological notion
of "free choice." That is to say, although the large majority of
the so-called "ordinary people" were not properly acquainted
with the reform program, the medical lobby (twice as strong
as the infamous defense lobby!) succeeded in imposing on
the public the fundamental idea that, with universal healthcare free choice (in matters concerning medicine) will be
somehow threatened – against this purely fictional reference

to "free choice", all enumeration of "hard facts" (in Canada, healthcare is less expensive and more effective, with no less free choice, etc.) proved ineffective.

Here we are at the very nerve center of the liberal ideology: freedom of choice, grounded in the notion of the "psychological" subject endowed with propensities he or she strives to realize. This especially holds today, in the era of what sociologists like Ulrich Beck call "risk society,"[19] when the ruling ideology endeavors to sell us the insecurity caused by the dismantling of the Welfare State as the opportunity for new freedoms: you have to change jobs every year, relying on short-term contracts instead of a long-term stable appointment. Why not see it as the liberation from the constraints of a fixed job, as the chance to reinvent yourself again and again, to become aware of and realize hidden potentials of your personality? You can no longer rely on the standard health insurance and retirement plan, so that you have to opt for additional coverage for which you have to pay. Why not perceive it as an additional opportunity to choose: either better life now or long-term security? And if this predicament causes you anxiety, the postmodern or "second modernity" ideologist will immediately accuse you of being unable to assume full freedom, of the "escape from freedom," of the immature sticking to old stable forms . . . Even better, when this is inscribed into the ideology of the subject as the psychological individual pregnant with natural abilities and tendencies, then I as it were automatically interpret all these changes as the results of my personality, not as the result of me being thrown around by market forces.

Phenomena like these make it all the more necessary today to REASSERT the opposition of "formal" and "actual" freedom in a new, more precise, sense. What we need today, in the era of liberal hegemony, is a "Leninist" *traité de la servitude liberale*, a new version of la Boétie's *Traité de la servitude volontaire* that would fully justify the apparent oxymoron "liberal totalitarianism." In experimental psychology, Jean-Léon Beauvois took the first step in this direction with his precise exploration of the paradoxes of conferring on the subject the freedom to choose.[20] Repeated experiments established the following paradox: if, AFTER getting from two groups of volunteers the agreement to participate in an experiment, one informs them that the experiment will involve something unpleasant, against their ethics even, and if, at this point, one reminds the first group that they have the free choice to say no, and says nothing to the other group, in BOTH groups, the SAME (very high) percentage will agree to continue their participation in the experiment.

What this means is that *conferring the formal freedom of choice does not make any difference*: those given the freedom will do the same thing as those (implicitly) denied it. This, however, does not mean that the reminder/bestowal of the freedom of choice does not make any difference: those given the freedom to choose will not only tend to choose the same as those denied it; they will tend to "rationalize" their "free" decision to continue to participate in the experiment – unable to endure the so-called cognitive dissonance (their awareness that they FREELY acted against their interests, propensities, tastes or norms), they will tend to *change their opinion* about the act they were asked to accomplish.

Let us say that an individual is first asked to participate in an experiment that concerns changing eating habits in order to fight against famine; then, after agreeing to do it, at the first encounter in the laboratory, he will be asked to swallow a living worm, with the explicit reminder that, if he finds this act repulsive, he can, of course, say no, since he has the complete freedom to choose. In most cases, he will do it, and then rationalize it by way of saying to himself something like: "What I am asked to do IS disgusting, but I am not a coward, I should display some courage and self-control, otherwise scientists will perceive me as a weak person who pulls out at the first minor obstacle! Furthermore, a worm does have a lot of proteins and it could effectively be used to feed the poor – who am I to hinder such an important experiment because of my petty sensitivity? And, finally, maybe my disgust of worms is just a prejudice, maybe a worm is not so bad – and would tasting it not be a new and daring experience? What if it will enable me to discover an unexpected, slightly perverse, dimension of myself that I was hitherto unaware of?"

Beauvois enumerates three modes of what brings people to accomplish such an act which runs against their perceived propensities and/or interests: *authoritarian* (the pure command "You should do it because I say so, without questioning it!", sustained by the reward if the subject does it and the punishment if he does not do it), *totalitarian* (the reference to some higher Cause or common Good which is larger than the subject's perceived interest: "You should do it because, even if it is unpleasant, it serves our Nation, Party, Humanity!"), and *liberal* (the reference to the subject's inner nature itself: "What is asked of you may appear repulsive, but look deep into yourself and you will discover that it's in your true nature to do it, you will find it attractive, you will become aware of new, unexpected, dimensions of your personality!").

At this point, Beauvois should be corrected: a direct authoritarianism is practically nonexistent – even the most oppressive regime *publicly* legitimizes its reign with the reference to some Higher Good, and the fact that, ultimately, "you have to obey because I say so" reverberates only as its obscene supplement discernible between the lines. It is rather the specificity of the standard authoritarianism to refer to some higher Good ("whatever your inclinations are, you have to follow my order for the sake of the higher Good!"), while totalitarianism, like liberalism, interpellates the subject on behalf of HIS OWN good ("what may appear to you as an external pressure, is really the expression of your objective interests, of what you REALLY WANT without being aware of it!"). The difference between the two resides elsewhere: "totalitarianism" imposes on the subject his or her own good, even if it is against his or her will – recall King Charles' (in)famous statement: "If any shall be so foolishly unnatural as to oppose their king, their country and their own good, we will make them happy, by God's blessing – even against their wills."(Charles I to the Earl of Essex, 6 August 1644.) Here we encounter the later Jacobin theme of happiness as a political factor, as well as the Saint-Justian idea of forcing people to be happy . . . Liberalism tries to avoid (or, rather, cover up) this paradox by way of clinging to the end to the fiction of the subject's immediate free self-perception ("I don't claim to know better than you what you want – just look deep into yourself and decide freely what you want!").

The reason for this fault in Beauvois's line of argumentation is that he fails to recognize how the abyssal tautological authority ("It is so because I say so!" of the Master) does not work only because of the sanctions (punishment/reward) it implicitly or explicitly evokes. That is to say, what, effectively, makes a subject freely choose what is imposed on him against his interests and/or propensities? Here, the empirical inquiry into "pathological" (in the Kantian sense of the term) motivations is not sufficient: the enunciation of an injunction that imposes on its addressee a symbolic engagement/commitment evinces an inherent force of its own, so that what seduces us into obeying it is the very feature that may appear to be an obstacle – the absence of a "why." Here, Lacan can be of some help: the Lacanian "Master-Signifier" designates precisely this hypnotic force of the symbolic injunction which relies only on its own act of enunciation – it is here that we encounter "symbolic efficiency" at its purest. The three ways of legitimizing the exercise of authority ("authoritarian," "totalitarian," "liberal") are nothing but three ways of covering up, of blinding us to the seductive power of the abyss of this empty call. In a way, liberalism is here even the worst of the three, since it NATURALIZES the reasons for obedience into the subject's internal psychological structure. So the paradox is that "liberal" subjects are in a way those least free: they change the very opinion/perception of themselves, accepting what was IMPOSED on them as originating in their "nature" – they are even no longer AWARE of their subordination.

Let us take the situation in the Eastern European countries around 1990, when Really Existing Socialism was falling apart: all of a sudden, people were thrown into a situation of the "freedom of political choice" – however, were they REALLY at any point asked the fundamental question of what kind of new order they actually wanted? Is it not that they found themselves in the exact situation of the subject–victim of a Beauvois experiment? They were first told that they were entering the promised land of political freedom; then, soon afterwards, they were informed that this freedom involved wild privatization, the dismantling of the system of social security, etc. etc. – they still have the freedom to choose, so if they want, they can step out; but, no, our heroic Eastern

Europeans didn't want to disappoint their Western mentors, they stoically persisted in the choice they never made, convincing themselves that they should behave as mature subjects who are aware that freedom has its price . . . This is why the notion of the psychological subject endowed with natural propensities, who has to realize its true Self and its potentials, and who is, consequently, ultimately responsible for his failure or success, is the key ingredient of liberal freedom. And here one should risk reintroducing the Leninist opposition of "formal" and "actual" freedom: in an act of actual freedom, one dares precisely to BREAK the seductive power of symbolic efficiency. Therein resides the moment of truth of Lenin's acerbic retort to his Menshevik critics: the truly free choice is a choice in which I do not merely choose between two or more options WITHIN a pre-given set of coordinates, but I choose to change this set of coordinates itself. The catch of the "transition" from Really Existing Socialism to capitalism was that people never had the chance to choose the *ad quem* of this transition – all of a sudden, they were (almost literally) "thrown" into a new situation in which they were presented with a new set of given choices (pure liberalism, nationalist conservatism . . .). What this means is that the "actual freedom" as the act of consciously changing this set occurs only when, in the situation of a forced choice, one ACTS AS IF THE CHOICE IS NOT FORCED and "chooses the impossible."

This is what Lenin's obsessive tirades against "formal" freedom are about, therein resides their "rational kernel" which is worth saving today: when he emphasizes that there is no "pure" democracy, that we should always ask who does a freedom under consideration serve, which is its role in the class struggle, his point is precisely to maintain the possibility of the TRUE radical choice. This is what the distinction between "formal" and "actual" freedom ultimately amounts to: "formal" freedom is the freedom of choice WITHIN the coordinates of the existing power relations, while "actual" freedom designates the site of an intervention which undermines these very coordinates. In short, Lenin's point is not to limit freedom of choice, but to maintain the fundamental Choice — when Lenin asks about the role of a freedom within the class struggle, what he is asking is precisely: "Does this freedom contribute to or constrain the fundamental revolutionary Choice?"

The most popular TV show of the fall of 2000 in France, with the viewer rating two times higher than that of the notorious "Big Brother" reality soaps, was "C'est mon choix" ("It is my choice") on France 3, the talkshow whose guest is an ordinary (or, exceptionally, a well-known) person who made a peculiar choice which determined his or her entire life-style: one of them decided never to wear underwear, another tries to find a more appropriate sexual partner for his father and mother — extravagance is allowed, solicited even, but with the explicit exclusion of the choices which may disturb the public (for example, a person whose choice is to be and act as a racist, is a priori excluded). Can one imagine a better predicament of what the "freedom of choice" effectively amounts to in our liberal societies? We can go on making our small choices, "reinventing ourselves" thoroughly, on condition that these choices do not seriously disturb the social and ideological balance. For "C'est mon choix," the truly radical thing would have been to focus precisely on the "disturbing" choices: to invite as guests people like dedicated racists, i.e. people whose choice (whose difference) DOES make a difference. This, also, is the reason why, today, "democracy" is more and more a false issue, a notion so discredited by its predominant use that, perhaps, one should take the risk of abandoning it to the enemy. Where, how, by whom are the key decisions concerning global social issues made? Are they made in the public space, through the engaged participation of the majority? If the answer is yes, it is of secondary importance if the state has a one-party system, etc. If the answer is no, it is of secondary importance if we have parliamentary democracy and freedom of individual choice.

Did something homologous to the invention of the liberal psychological individual not take place in the Soviet Union in the late 1920s and early 1930s? The Russian avant-garde art of the early 1920s (futurism, constructivism) not only zealously endorsed industrialization, it even endeavored to reinvent a new industrial man – no longer the old man of sentimental passions and roots in traditions, but the new man who gladly accepts his role as a bolt or screw in the gigantic coordinated industrial Machine. As such, it was subversive in its very "ultra-orthodoxy," i.e. in its over-identification with the core of the official ideology: the image of man that we get in Eisenstein, Meyerhold, constructivist paintings, etc., emphasizes the beauty of his/her mechanical movements, his/her thorough depsychologization. What was perceived in the West as the ultimate nightmare of liberal individualism, as the ideological counterpoint to "Taylorization," to Fordist ribbon-work, was in Russia hailed as the *utopian* prospect of liberation: recall how Meyerhold violently asserted the "behaviorist" approach to acting – no longer emphatic familiarization with the person the actor is playing, but ruthless bodily training aimed at cold bodily discipline, at the ability of the actor to perform a series of mechanized movements . . .[21] THIS is what was unbearable to AND IN the official Stalinist ideology, so that the Stalinist "socialist realism" effectively WAS an attempt to reassert a "Socialism with a human face," i.e. to reinscribe the process of industrialization within the constraints of the traditional psychological individual: in the Socialist Realist texts, paintings and films, individuals are no longer rendered as parts of the global Machine, but as warm, passionate persons.

The obvious reproach that imposes itself here is, of course: is the basic characteristic of today's "postmodern" subject not the exact opposite of the free subject who experienced himself as ultimately responsible for his fate, namely the subject who grounds the authority of his speech on his status of a victim of circumstances beyond his control? Every contact with another human being is experienced as a potential threat – if the other smokes, if he casts a covetous glance at me, he already hurts me; this logic of victimization is today universalized, reaching well beyond the standard cases of sexual or racist harassment – recall the growing financial industry of paying damage claims, from the tobacco industry deal in the USA and the financial claims of the Holocaust victims and forced laborers in Nazi Germany, and the idea that the USA should pay the African-Americans hundreds of billions of dollars for all they were deprived of due to their past slavery . . . This notion of the subject as an irresponsible victim involves the extreme Narcissistic perspective from which every encounter with the Other appears as a potential threat to the subject's precarious imaginary balance; as such, it is not the opposite, but, rather, the inherent supplement of the liberal free subject: in today's predominant form of individuality, the self-centered assertion of the psychological subject paradoxically overlaps with the perception of oneself as a victim of circumstances.

Badiou himself gets caught here in the proto-Kantian trap of "spurious infinity": afraid of the potential "totalitarian" terrorist consequences of asserting "actual freedom" as the direct inscription of the Event into the order of Being (was Stalinism not precisely such a direct "ontologization" of the Event, its reduction to a new positive order of Being?), he emphasizes the gap that separates them forever. For Badiou, fidelity to the Event involves the work of discerning its traces, the work which is by definition never done; in spite of all claims to the contrary, he thus relies on a kind of the Kantian regulative Idea, on the final end (the full conversion of the Event into Being) which one can only approach in an endless process. Although Badiou emphatically advocates the return to philosophy, he thereby nonetheless displays the failure to grasp the fundamental authentically *philosophical* insight, shared by Hegel and Nietzsche, his great opponent – does Nietzsche's "eternal return of the same" not point in the same direction as the very last words of Hegel's *Encyclopaedia*: "The eternal Idea, in full fruition of its essence, eternally sets itself to work, engendering and enjoying itself as absolute Spirit?"[22] For an authentic philosopher, *everything has always–already happened*; what is difficult to grasp is how this notion not only does NOT prevent engaged activity, but effectively SUSTAINS it. The famous Jesuit axiom concerning human activity displays a clear presentiment of this insight:

> Here, then, is the first rule of acting: assume/believe that the success of your undertakings depends entirely on you, and in no way on God; but, nonetheless, set to work as if God alone will do everything, and you yourself nothing.[23]

This axiom reverts the common maxim to which it is usually reduced: "Help yourself and God will help you!" (i.e.,

"Believe that God guides your hand, but act as if everything depends on you!"). The difference is crucial here: you must experience yourself as fully responsible – the trust in God must be in your ACTS, not in your BELIEFS. While the common maxim involves the standard fetishist split of "I know very well [that everything depends on me], but nonetheless ... [I believe in God's helping hand]," the Jesuit version is not a simple symmetrical reversal of this split – it rather thoroughly undermines the logic of the fetishist disavowal.

The political aspect of this gap is, of course, Badiou's marginalist anti-Statism: authentic politics should shun active involvement with State power, it should restrain itself to an agency of pure declarations which formulate the unconditional demands of *égaliberté*. Badiou's politics thus comes dangerously close to an apolitical politics – the very opposite of, say, Lenin's ruthless readiness to seize power and impose a new political order. (At the most radical level, the deadlock Badiou is dealing with here concerns the thorough ambiguity of what he calls l'*innommable*, "the unnameable": what cannot be named is SIMULTANEOUSLY the Event prior to its Nomination AND the senseless factuality, givenness, of the pure multitude of Being – from the Hegelian standpoint, they are ultimately THE SAME, since it is the act of nomination itself which retroactively elevates some feature of Being into the Event.)

This brings us back to Judaism and Christianity: Jews wait for the arrival of their Messiah, their attitude is one of suspended attention directed towards the future, while, for a Christian believer, *the Messiah is already here*, the Event has already taken place. How, then, does Judaism "mediate" between paganism and Christianity?[24] In a way, it is already in Judaism that we find the "unplugging" from the immersion into the

Cosmic Order, into the Chain of Being, i.e. the direct access to universality as opposed to the global Order, which is the basic feature of Christianity. This is the ultimate meaning of Exodus: the withdrawal from the hierarchized (Egyptian) Order under the impact of the direct divine call.[25]

WHY THE JEWISH ICONOCLASM?

How, then, are we to understand the Jewish subordination to the laws of the country in which they live as exiles? Their specific existence disturbs the standard tension between the symbolic Law and its obscene superego supplement. Far from being the nation of (the superego) GUILT, Jews are precisely LIBERATED from its pressure. THIS is the reason why, without falling into the superego trap, Jews can search for ways to retain the desired object while obeying literally the Law – they don't feel guilty, they don't cheat, since there is nothing "behind" the law. Therein resides the uncanniness of the Jewish position: they ONLY stick to the SYMBOLIC RULES, deprived of the obscene fantasmatic background. There is no place in Judaism for the private wink of understanding, no obscene solidarity about their shared complicity among the perpetrators of the transgression. In other words, Jews are truly "cosmopolitan" – they are not ENJOYING their national identity, they have no sensitivity for "blood and soil," for their "roots." Their homeland is forever postponed, infinitized ("Next year in Jerusalem!"). However, this liberation from the superego confronts the Jews even more directly with the trauma of the encounter of the Thing, with the excessive over-excitation which is no longer domesticated into "national substance," but retains its extimate character.

The paradox of the Jewish identity is that its position – the position of "universal singularity," of the homeless, exiled, outcast of nations, which directly stands for the nationhood "as such" – takes the form of a series of arbitrary particular rules (kosher food, etc.) which defines a specific ETHNIC community. The cutting loose from a particular ethnic identity takes the form of ethnicity itself (in a homologous way, rejection of bodily cuts takes the form of circumcision[26]): Jews form the "community which is none" (homologous to Luce Irigaray's determination of women as *le sexe qui n'est pas un*). To put it in Jacques Rancière's terms,[27] Jews stand for the universality of humankind precisely insofar as they do not have a proper place in the order of particular races, insofar as they are a remainder that doesn't fit into this order. The immediate counter-argument to this idea is, of course, that Jews not only DO display a whole set of specific practices that distinguish them from the Gentiles, but that they even put a much stronger accent on these practices than other ethnic groups. However, WHY do Jews have to regulate everything through negotiated rules? Is it not because they effectively ARE "rootless" in a much more radical sense than even anti-Semitism dares to impute to them? In a way, they effectively do not live in what communitarians today refer to as "life-world": they lack the thick impenetrable background cobweb of implicit presuppositions, rituals, unwritten rules, enacted practices, which cannot ever be objectivized into the set of explicit norms – their "life-world" is artificially negotiated and constructed. Maybe, a Wittgensteinian division between saying and showing can be of some use here: Christianity involves the distinction between external rules and inner belief (so the question is always: do you REALLY, in the innermost of your heart, believe, or are you just following the dead letter of the law?), while in Judaism, the "external" rules and practices DIRECTLY ARE the religious belief in its material existence –

Jews do not have to DECLARE their belief, they immediately SHOW it in their practice. Which is why Christianity is the religion of inner turmoil, of self-examination, while for Judaism, the problems are ultimately those of the "external" legalistic discourse – Jews focus on the rules to be followed, questions of "inner belief" are simply not raised.

Jews thus enact the necessity of a mediatory figure: in order to break through, the New must first express itself in the old form (as Marx himself pointed out apropos of modernity: the break with the medieval religious universe has first to take the form of a religious heresy, i.e. of Protestantism). In Hegelese: perhaps, Judaism and Christianity are related as In-itself and For-itself – Judaism is Christianity "in itself," still in the form of paganism, articulated in the pagan horizon. *Within* this horizon (of images, sexualized rituals, etc.), the New can only assert itself in the guise of a radical prohibition: no images, no sacred orgies. Or, with regard to ethnicity: within the ethnic space, the New can only articulate itself as the paradox of a "supernumerary" community with no roots, no land, forever in search of it, wandering around . . . On the other hand, what this means is that Christianity is merely Judaism "for itself."

So what about the Jewish assertion of the unconditional iconoclastic monotheism: God is One, totally Other, with no human form? The commonplace position is here that pagan (pre-Jewish) gods were "anthropomorphic" (say, old Greek gods fornicated, cheated, and engaged in other ordinary human passions), while the Jewish religion, with its iconoclasm, was the first to thoroughly "de-anthropomorphize" divinity. What, however, if things are the exact opposite? What if the very need to prohibit man from making the images of God bears witness to the "personification" of God discernible in "Let us make humankind in our image, according to our likeness" (*Genesis* 1: 26) – what if the true target of Jewish iconoclastic prohibition is not previous pagan religions, but rather its *own* "anthropomorphization"/ "personalization" of God? What if the Jewish religion *itself* generates the excess it has to prohibit? It is the JEWISH God who is the FIRST fully "personalized" God, a God who says "I am who I am." In other words, iconoclasm and other Jewish prohibitions do not relate to the pagan Otherness, but to the violence of Judaism's OWN imaginary excess – in pagan religions, such prohibition would have been simply *meaningless*. Making images has to be prohibited not because of the pagans; its true reason is the premonition that, if the Jews were to do the same as the pagans, something horrible would have emerged (the hint of this horror is given in Freud's hypothesis about the murder of Moses, this traumatic event on the denial of which the Jewish identity is raised).[28] The prohibition against making images is therefore equivalent to the Jewish disavowal of the primordial crime: the primordial parricide is the ultimate fascinating image.[29] (What, then, does the Christian reassertion of the unique *image* of the crucified Christ stand for?)[30]

Anthropomorphism and iconoclasm are thus NOT simple opposites: it is NOT that pagan religions depict gods as simple "larger than life" human persons, while Judaism prohibits such a depiction. It is only with Judaism that God is FULLY "anthropomorphized," that the encounter with Him is the encounter with another PERSON in the fullest sense of the term – the Jewish God experiences full wrath, revengefulness, jealousy, etc., as every human being ... THIS is why one is prohibited to make images of Him: not because an image would "humanize" the purely spiritual Entity, but because it would render it all too faithfully, as the ultimate

Neighbor-Thing.[31] Christianity only goes to the end in this direction by asserting not only the likeness of God and man, but their direct identity in the figure of Christ: "no wonder man looks like God, since a man (Christ) IS God." With its central notion of Christ as man–God, Christianity just makes "for itself" the personalization of God in Judaism. According to the standard notion, pagans were anthropomorphic, Jews were radically iconoclastic, and Christianity accomplishes a kind of "synthesis," a partial regression to paganism, by introducing the ultimate "icon to erase all other icons," that of the suffering Christ. Against this commonplace, one should assert that it is the Jewish religion which remains an "abstract/immediate" negation of anthropomorphism, and, as such, attached to it, determined by it in its very direct negation, whereas it is only Christianity that effectively "sublates" paganism.[32] The Christian stance is here: instead of prohibiting the image of God, why not, precisely, allow it, and thus render him as JUST ANOTHER HUMAN BEING, as a miserable man indiscernible from other humans with regard to his intrinsic properties?

If one is permitted to indulge in a sacrilegious parallel, science-fiction horror movies practice two modes to render the Alien Thing: either the Thing is wholly Other, a monster whose sight one cannot endure, usually a mixture of reptile, octopus and machine (like the Alien from Ridley Scott's film of the same name), or it is EXACTLY THE SAME as we, ordinary humans – with, of course, some "barely nothing" which allows us to identify Them (the strange gleam in their eyes; too much skin between their fingers . . .). Christ is fully a man only insofar as he takes upon himself the excess/remainder, the "too much" on account of which a man, precisely, is never fully a man: his formula is not Man=God, but man=man, where the divine dimension intervenes only as that "something" which prevents man from attaining his full identity. In this sense, Christ's appearance itself effectively stands for God's death: in it, it becomes clear that God is NOTHING BUT the excess of man, the "too much" of life which cannot be contained in any life-form, which violates the shape (*morphe*) of anthropomorphism.

To put it even more directly: pagans were NOT celebrating images, they were well aware that the images they were making remained inadequate copies of the true Divinity (recall the old Hindu statues of Gods with dozens of hands, etc. – a clear example of how any attempt to render Divinity in a sensual/material form fails by way of turning into a half-ridiculous exaggeration). In contrast to the pagans, it was the Jews themselves who believed/assumed that the (sensual/material) image of the divine Person would show too much, rendering visible some horrifying secret better left in shadow, WHICH IS WHY THEY HAD TO PROHIBIT IT – the Jewish prohibition only makes sense against the background of this fear that the image would reveal something shattering, that, in an unbearable way, it would be TRUE and ADEQUATE. The same goes for the Christians: when Saint Augustine opposed Christianity, the religion of Love, to Judaism, the religion of Anxiety, when he conceived of the passage from Judaism to Christianity as the passage from Anxiety to Love, he (again) projected onto Judaism the disavowed founding gesture of Christianity itself – what Christianity endeavors to overcome through the reconciliation in Love is *its own constitutive excess*, the unbearable anxiety opened up by the experience of the impotent God who failed in His work of creation, i.e., to refer yet again to Hegel, the traumatic experience of how the enigma of God is also the enigma for God Himself – our failure to comprehend God is what Hegel called a "reflexive determination" of the divine self-limitation.

And the same goes for the standard opposition between the Cartesian self-transparent subject of thought and the Freudian subject of the unconscious, which is perceived as anti-Cartesian, as undermining the Cartesian "illusion" of rational identity. One should bear in mind that the opposite by reference to which a certain position asserts itself is ITS OWN presupposition, its own inherent excess (as is the case with Kant: the notion of diabolical Evil which he rejects is only possible within the horizon of HIS OWN transcendental revolution). The point here is not so much that the Cartesian cogito is the presupposed "vanishing mediator" of the Freudian subject of the unconscious (a thought worth pursuing), but that the subject of the unconscious is already operative in the Cartesian cogito as its own inherent excess: in order to assert cogito as the self-transparent "thinking substance," one HAS to pass through the excessive point of madness which designates cogito as the vanishing abyss of substanceless thought. Along the same lines, the Jewish–Christian openness to the Other ("Love thy neighbor!") is thoroughly different from the pagan tribal hospitality: while pagan hospitality relies on the clear opposition between the self-enclosed domain of my community and the external Other, what reverberates in the Jewish–Christian openness is a reaction against the traumatic recognition of *the neighbor as the unfathomable abyssal Thing* – the Alien Thing is my closest neighbor himself, not the foreigner visiting my home. In Hegelese, the Jewish–Christian openness involves the logic of "positing its presuppositions": it instigates us to remain open towards the Otherness which is experienced as such only within its own horizon.

Kant and Freud both claim to repeat the "Copernican turn" in their respective domains. With regard to Freud, the meaning of this reference seems clear and simple: in the same way that Copernicus demonstrated that our Earth is not the center of the universe, but a planet revolving around the Sun, and in this sense "decentered," turning around *another* center, Freud also demonstrated that the (conscious) Ego is not the center of the human psyche, but ultimately an epiphenomenon, a satellite turning around the true center, the Unconscious or the Id . . . With Kant, things are more ambiguous – in a first approach, it cannot but appear that he actually did the exact *opposite* of the Copernican turn: is not the key premise of his transcendental approach that the conditions of possibility of our experience of the objects are at the same time the conditions of possibility of these objects themselves, so that, instead of a subject who, in his cognition, has to accommodate itself to some external, "decentered," measure of truth, the objects have to follow the subject, i.e. it is the subject itself who, from its central position, constitutes the objects of knowledge? However, if one reads Kant's reference to Copernicus closely, one cannot fail to notice how Kant's emphasis is not on the shift of the substantial fixed Center, but on something quite different – on the status of the subject itself:

> We here propose to do just what Copernicus did in attempting to explain the celestial movements. When he found that he could make no progress by assuming that all the heavenly bodies revolved round the spectator, he reversed the process, and tried the experiment of assuming that the spectator revolved, while the stars remained at rest.[33]

The precise German terms ("die Zuschauer sich drehen" – not so much turn around another center as turn/*rotate around themselves*)[34] make it clear what interests Kant: the subject loses its substantial stability/identity and is reduced to the pure substanceless void of the self-rotating abyssal vortex called "transcendental apperception." And it is against this background that one can locate Lacan's "return to Freud": to put it as succinctly as possible, what Lacan does is to read the Freudian reference to the Copernican turn *in the original Kantian sense*, as asserting not the simple displacement of the center from the Ego to the Id or the Unconscious as the "true" substantial focus of the human psyche, but the transformation of the subject itself from the self-identical substantial Ego, the psychological subject full of emotions, instincts, dispositions, etc., to what Lacan called the "barred subject ($)," the vortex of the self-relating negativity of desire. In this precise sense, the subject of the unconscious is none other than the Cartesian *cogito*.

The same logic of "reflexive determination" is at work in the passage from revolutionary Terror (absolute Freedom) to the Kantian moral subject in Hegel's *Phenomenology*: the revolutionary subject experiences himself as mercilessly exposed to the whim of the terrorist regime – anyone can at any moment be arrested and put to death as "traitor." Of course, the passage to moral subjectivity occurs when this external terror is internalized by the subject as the terror of the moral law, of the voice of conscience. However, what is often overlooked is that, in order for this internalization to take place, the subject has to profoundly transform his identity: he has to renounce the very kernel of his contingent individuality, and to accept that the center of his identity resides in his universal moral consciousness. In other words, it is only insofar as I cling to my contingent idiosyncratic identity as to the core of my being that I experience the universal Law as the abstract negativity of an alien power that threatens to annihilate me; in this precise sense, the internalization of the Law is merely the "reflexive determination" of the shift that affects the core of my own identity. It is not the Law which changes from the agency of external political Terror to the pressure of the inner voice of conscience; this change merely reflects the change in my identity. Perhaps, something similar occurs in the passage from Judaism to Christianity: what changes in this passage is not the content (the status of God), but primarily the identity of the believer him/herself, and the change in God (no longer the transcendent Other, but Christ) is just the reflexive determination of THIS change.

Is this not also the implicit lesson of Thomas Hobbes' key insight apropos of the social contract? In order to be effective, the *limitation* of individuals' sovereignty – when they agree to transpose it onto the figure of the Sovereign and thus end up the state of war and introduce civic peace – must bestow *unlimited* power to the person of the Sovereign. It is not enough to have the rule of the laws on which we all agree and which then regulate the interaction between individuals in order to avoid the war of all against all that characterizes the state of nature: in order for the laws to be operative, there must be a One, a person with the unlimited power to DECIDE what are the laws. Mutually recognized rules are not enough – there must be a Master to enforce them. Therein resides the properly *dialectical* paradox of Hobbes: he starts with the individual's unlimited right to self-preservation, contained by no duties (I have the unalienable right to cheat, steal, lie, kill . . . if my survival is at stake), and he ends up with the Sovereign who has the unlimited power to dispose of my life, the Sovereign whom I experience not as the extension of my own will, as the personification of my ethical substance, but as an arbitrary foreign force. This external unlimited power is precisely the reflexive determination of my "egotist" subjective stance – the way to overcome it is to change MY OWN identity.

AUTHOR, SUBJECT, EXECUTIONER

So how are Judaism and Christianity related? The standard Judeo–Lacanian answer is that Christianity is a kind of regression to the imaginary narcissistic fusion of the community that forsakes the traumatic tension between Law and sin (its transgression). Consequently, Christianity replaces the logic of Exodus, of an open-ended voyage without any guarantee as to its final outcome, with the messianic logic of the final reconciliation – the idea of the "perspective of Last Judgement" is foreign to Judaism. Along these lines, Eric Santner is fully justified in claiming that, while Judaism is a religion whose public discourse is haunted by the spectral shadow of its obscene uncanny double, of its excessive transgressive founding violent gesture (it is this very disavowed attachment to the traumatic kernel which confers on Judaism its extraordinary chutzpah and durability), Christianity does not possess *another*, its own, obscene disavowed supplement, but simply *has none*.[35] The Christian answer is that, precisely, *the tension between the pacifying Law and the excessive superego is not the ultimate horizon of our experience*: it is possible to step out of this domain, not into the fake imaginary bliss, but into the Real of an act; it is possible to cut the Gordian knot of transgression and guilt. Antigone is thus effectively the precursor of a Christian figure, insofar as there is no tension whatsoever in her position between Law and transgression, between transgression and guilt, between the unconditional ethical demand and her inadequate answer to it.

Let us specify further this paradoxical position of Christ with reference to the Kantian ethical subject. When, in his "Kant avec Sade," Lacan claims that Kant – in his notion of the moral agent as the autonomous subject, the subject who posits his own moral law – obfuscates the division of the subject,[36] one should be very careful not to miss what he aims at: it is NOT the simple notion that Kant wrongly locates the origin of the moral Law in the subject itself, while this Law is effectively experienced by the subject as the voice of a foreign superego authority exerting on the subject an unbearable pressure. One should, rather, introduce here the distinction between THREE elements: the author of the moral Law, the subject who (has to) obey(s) the Law, AND the Law's EXECUTIONER/EXECUTOR – the one who executes the Law, and in whom Lacan discerns the contours of the Sadean executioner/torturer.[37] The problem is not the identity of the Law's author and subject: they effectively ARE the same, the subject effectively IS autonomous in the sense of obeying his/ her OWN Law; the problem resides in the supplementary figure of the Law's executioner/executor, who interposes itself, mediating between the subject as the Law's author and the subject as, precisely, the Law's subject. Referring to the well-known ambiguity of the very term "subject," out of which Louis Althusser and his followers drew a lot of theoretical mileage (the subject as autonomous agent; the subject of the Law and/or of a sovereign Power), the Sadean executioner's role is precisely to mediate between these two dimensions. And it was this dimension of the executor as the *objet petit a*, which supplements the dyad of the author of the law and its subject/"victim" with the third, mediating, element, this dimension of the pure *object/instrument*, not the subject, of the Law, that was overlooked by Kant, and introduced only by Sade – why? Because its status is neither formal–transcendental nor empirical: the executioner is a contingent "pathological" stain, yet a paradoxical stain whose status is nonetheless a priori, i.e. who is needed as the "pathological" support of this very transcendental dimension. Let's make this clear apropos of Stalinist Communism, whose structure is that of the Sadean perversion: in the Stalinist universe, we have the author of the Law (History itself, imposing on us the "eternal laws of inexorable progress towards Communism"), the subjects of this Law ("common" people, masses), AND the Communist Party, the pure object–instrument, executor, of the historical progress. And, *exactly as in Kant and Sade*, the split is not between the author and the subject of the Law – they are IDENTICAL, the "People," the "Masses" – but between the People as the author/subject of the Law of History *and its executor*, the (Communist) Party, the pure INSTRUMENT of historical Necessity which, in the mode of the Sadean executioner, bridges the gap between the transcendental and the empirical by way of terrorizing the (empirical) people *in its own name*, on behalf of its own (transcendental) destination.

What Kant and Sade unexpectedly share is the abyss which separates the chain of "pathological" (empirical) causes and effects from the pure Will ("I want it, irrespective of circumstances, even if all hell will break loose!"). In a first approach, the Kantian ethical Will obeying the imperative of universality cannot but appear as the radical opposite of the utter caprice which characterizes the Sadean pervert ("I want [this specific pleasure] because I want it, it is a pure caprice of mine, I don't have to justify it!").[38] However, this intrusion of pure caprice suspends the enchainment of causes and effects: the Sadean subject does not "rationalize," he never justifies or legitimizes his capricious demands – and does the same not hold also for the Kantian ethical subject who pursues his Duty irrespective of the constraining circumstances ("You can, because you must!"). This, then, is what, in the supreme dialectical coincidence, the universal Will striving to get rid of all "pathological" motivations, and the singular, absolutely capricious, Will share: the purity of Will uncontaminated by the utilitarian calculus of pleasures or profits. Both the Kantian ethical subject and the Sadean subject of the unreserved will to *jouissance* want what they want unconditionally and pursue it without regard to any utilitarian "rational" considerations. In this precise sense, as was clear to Hegel, the utter caprice is the hidden "truth" of the Kantian ethical universality – no wonder that Kant himself characterized the moral Law as a "*fact* of the practical reason," as an inexplicable unconditional demand which simply is there, exerting on us its unbearable pressure.

Back to Christianity: does this mean that Christ, this ultimate *objet petit a*, is also the same mediator between the Divine Law and its human subjects? Is his sacrifice for our sins of the same order as the proverbial Stalinist cadre's sacrifice for the progress of humanity? Is Christ's love for humanity structurally the same as the Communist leader's proverbial love for his people? Here, the difference is crucial: Christ no longer functions as an executioner with regard to the Law – he, on the contrary, *suspends* the dimension of the Law, signalling its *demise*. So, perhaps, the difference between Judaism and Christianity is, to put it in Schelling's terms, the difference between contraction and expansion: Jewish contraction (perseverance, enduring in the status of a remainder) lays the ground for the Christian expansion (love). If Jews assert the Law without superego, Christians assert love as *jouissance* outside the Law.

In order to get at *jouissance* outside Law, not tainted by the obscene superego supplement of the Law, the Law itself has first to be delivered from the grip of *jouissance*. The position to adopt between Judaism and Christianity is thus not simply to give preference to one of them, even less to opt for a kind of pseudo-dialectical "synthesis," but to introduce the gap between the enunciated content and the position of enunciation: as to the content of the belief, one should be a Jew, while retaining the Christian position of enunciation.[39]

There is an effective argument against our reading of Christianity: did (and does) it not, in its *historical actuality*, function in accordance with the logic of sacrificial exchange, with Christ paying for our sins and thus establishing itself as the ultimate superego figure to whom we are condemned to remain forever indebted? And, *mutatis mutandis*, does the same not hold for Judaism? Does the split between the "official" texts of the Law with their abstract legal asexual character (Torah – the Old Testament – Mishna – the formulation of the Laws – and Talmud – the commentary of the Laws – all of them supposed to be part of the Divine Revelation on Mount Sinai), and Kabbalah (this set of deeply sexualized obscure insights to be kept secret – recall the notorious passages about the vaginal juices) not reproduce *within* Judaism the tension between the pure symbolic Law and its superego supplement, the secret initiatic knowledge? The key question here is: which, exactly, is Kabbalah's status within Judaism? Is it perceived as its necessary and inherent obscene supplement, or merely as a heretic deviation against which one should fight (in the same way Christianity has to fight against Gnostic heresies)? Most of the evidence seems to point towards the first option: Kabbalah is the INHERENT obscene supplement to the Law, something about which one does not talk in public, something that one prefers shamefully to avoid, and which, nonetheless, on that very account provides the phantasmic core of the Jewish identity. What further complicates the picture is that Kabbalah is not the only publicly "unmentionable" Jewish religious text: in some versions of the Talmud, the very relationship between Torah and Talmud resembles the later Catholic attitude towards the Bible (or, incidentally, the Stalinist attitude towards the texts of the "classics": Marx, Engels, Lenin) – it is prohibited to read it directly, bypassing the proper commentaries provided by the Church (or, in the case of Stalinism, the Party), since the direct reading can lead us astray, into a terrible heresy ... Along the same lines, a certain Talmudic tradition forbids quoting the Torah directly and verbatim: one is only allowed its learned commentaries.

It is thus only Christianity which effectively leaves this tension behind, insofar as it is able to fully renounce the need of the obscene supplement: there is no secret text accompanying as the superego shadow the Gospel. The solution is then that we should clearly identify in BOTH Judaism and Christianity a certain inherent tendency to "regress," to betray its innermost radical stance: in Judaism, the tendency to perceive God as the cruel superego figure; in Christianity, the tendency to reduce *agape* to an imaginary reconciliation which obfuscates the Otherness of the divine Thing. Which is why, perhaps, both Judaism and Christianity need the reference to each other to prevent this "regression."[40]

NO MERCY!

Herbert Schnädelbach's essay "Der Fluch des Christentums"[41] provides perhaps the most concise liberal attack on Christianity, enumerating its seven – not sins, but "birth-blunders":

(1) the notion of the original sin that pertains to humanity as such;

(2) the notion that God paid for that sin through a violent legal settlement with himself, sacrificing his own son;

(3) the missionary expansionism;

(4) anti-Semitism;

(5) eschatology with its vision of the final Day of Reckoning;

(6) the import of the Platonic dualism with its hatred of the body;

(7) the manipulative dealing with historical truth.

Although, in a predictable way, Schnädelbach puts most of the blame on St Paul, on his drive to institutionalize Christianity, he emphasizes that we are not dealing here with the secondary corruption of the original Christian teaching of love, but with the dimension present at its very origins. Furthermore, he insists that – to put it bluntly – all that is really worthwhile in Christianity (love, human dignity, etc.) is not specifically Christian, but was taken over into Christianity from Judaism.

What is perceived here as the problem is precisely the Christian *universalism*: what this all-inclusive attitude (recall St Paul's famous "There are no men or women, no Jews and Greeks") involves is a thorough exclusion of those who do not accept inclusion into the Christian community. In other "particularistic" religions (and even in Islam, in spite of its global expansionism), there is a place for others, they are tolerated, even if they are condescendingly looked upon. The Christian motto "All men are brothers," however, means ALSO that "Those who are not my brothers ARE NOT MEN." Christians usually praise themselves for overcoming the Jewish exclusivist notion of the Chosen People and encompassing all of humanity – the catch is here that, in their very insistence that they are the Chosen People with the privileged direct link to God, Jews accept the humanity of the other people who celebrate their false gods, while Christian universalism tendentially excludes non-believers from the very universality of humankind.

The question remains, nonetheless, if such a quick dismissal of Christianity does not fail to account for the momentous dimension of the Paulinian *agape* – the "miracle" of the retroactive "undoing" of sins through the suspension of the Law. One usually opposes here the rigorous Jewish Justice and Christian Mercy, the inexplicable gesture of undeserved pardon: we, humans, were born in sin, we cannot ever repay our debts and redeem ourselves through our own acts – our only salvation lies in God's Mercy, in His supreme sacrifice. In this very gesture of breaking the chain of Justice through the inexplicable act of Mercy, of paying our debt, Christianity imposes on us an even stronger debt: we are forever indebted to Christ, we cannot ever repay him for what he did for us. The Freudian name for such an excessive pressure which we cannot ever remunerate is, of course, *superego*.[42] (More precisely, the notion of Mercy is in itself ambiguous, so that it cannot fully be reduced to this superego agency: there is also Mercy in the sense Badiou reads this notion, namely the "mercy" of the Event of Truth (or, for Lacan, of the act) – we cannot actively decide to accomplish an act, the act surprises the agent itself, and "mercy" designated precisely this unexpected occurrence of an act.)

Usually, it is Judaism which is conceived as the religion of the superego (of man's subordination to the jealous, mighty and severe God), in contrast to the Christian God of Mercy and Love. However, it is precisely through NOT demanding from us the price for our sins, through paying this price for us Himself, that the Christian God of Mercy establishes itself as the supreme superego agency: "I paid the highest price for your sins, and you are thus indebted to me FOREVER . . . ". Is this God as the superego agency, whose very Mercy generates the indelible guilt of believers, the ultimate horizon of Christianity? Is the Christian *agape* another name for Mercy?

In order to properly locate Christianity with regard to this opposition, one should recall Hegel's famous dictum apropos of the Sphinx: "The enigmas of the Ancient Egyptians were enigmas also for the Egyptians themselves." Along the same lines, the elusive, impenetrable *Dieu obscur* has to be impenetrable also to Himself, He has to have a dark side, something that is in Him more than Himself. Perhaps, this accounts for the shift from Judaism to Christianity: Judaism remains at the level of the enigma OF God, while Christianity involves the move to the enigma IN God Himself. The Christian *logos*, the divine Revelation in and through the Word, and the enigma IN God are strictly correlative, two aspects of one and the same gesture. It is precisely because God is an enigma also IN AND FOR HIMSELF, because he has an unfathomable Otherness in Himself, that Christ had to emerge to reveal God not only to humanity, but TO GOD HIMSELF – it is only through Christ that God fully actualized himself as God.[43]

What is incomprehensible within the pre-Christian horizon is the full shattering dimension of this impenetrability of God to Himself, discernible in Christ's "Father, why did you forsake me?," this Christian version of the Freudian "Father, can't you see that I am burning?". This total abandonment by God is the point at which Christ becomes FULLY human, the point at which *the radical gap that separates God from man is transposed* into God Himself. Here, *God the Father Himself stumbles upon the limit of his omnipotence.* What this means is that the Christian notion of the link between man and God thus inverts the standard pagan notion according to which man approaches God through spiritual purification, through casting off the "low" material/sensual aspects of his being and thus elevating himself towards God. *When I, a human being, experience myself as cut off from God, at that very moment of the utmost abjection, I am absolutely close to God, since I find myself in the position of the abandoned Christ.* There is no "direct" identification with (or approach to) the divine majesty: I identify myself with God only through identifying myself with the unique figure of God-the-Son abandoned by God. In short, Christianity gives a specific twist to the story of Job, the man-believer abandoned by God – it is Christ (God) himself who has to occupy the place of Job. Man's identity with God is asserted only in/through God's radical self-abandonment, when his distance towards God overlaps with the inner distance of God towards himself. The only way for God to create free people (humans) is to open up the space for them in HIS OWN lack/void/gap: man's existence is the living proof of God's self-limitation. Or, to put it in more speculative–theological terms: man's infinite distance from God, the fact that he is a sinful, evil being, marked by the Fall, unworthy of God, has to be reflected back onto God himself, as the Evil of God the Father Himself, i.e. as his abandonment of his Son. Man's abandonment of God and God's abandonment of his Son are strictly correlative, the two aspects of one and the same gesture.

This divine self-abandonment, this impenetrability of God to Himself, thus signals God's fundamental *imperfection*. And it is only within this horizon that the properly Christian Love can emerge, a *Love beyond Mercy*. Love is always love for the

Other insofar as he is lacking – we love the Other BECAUSE of his limitation, helplessness, ordinariness even. In contrast to the pagan celebration of the Divine (or human) Perfection, the ultimate secret of the Christian love is, perhaps, the loving attachment to the Other's imperfection. It is this lack in/of the Other that opens up the space for the "good news" brought by Christianity. At the apogee of German Idealism, F.W.J. Schelling deployed the notion of the primordial decision–differentiation (*Ent-Scheidung*), the unconscious atemporal deed by means of which the subject chooses his/her eternal character which, afterwards, within his/her conscious–temporal life, is experienced as the inexorable necessity, as "the way s/he always was":

> The deed, once accomplished, sinks immediately into the unfathomable depth, thereby acquiring its lasting character. It is the same with the will which, once posited at the beginning and led into the outside, immediately has to sink into the unconscious. This is the only way the beginning, the beginning that does not cease to be one, the truly eternal beginning, is possible. For here also it holds that the beginning should not know itself. Once done, the deed is eternally done. The decision that is in any way the true beginning should not appear before consciousness, it should not be recalled to mind, since this, precisely, would amount to its recall. He who, apropos of a decision, reserves for himself the right to drag it again to light, will never accomplish the beginning.[44]

This absolute beginning is never made in the present: its status is that of a pure presupposition, of something which always–already took place. In other words, it is the paradox of a *passive decision*, of passively assuming the Decision that grounds our being as the supreme act of freedom – the paradox of the highest free choice which consists in assuming that one is chosen. In his *Adieu à Emmanuel Levinas*, Derrida tries to dissociate the decision from its usual metaphysical predicates (autonomy, consciousness, activity, sovereignty . . .) and think of it as the "other's decision in me":

> The passive decision, condition of the event, is always,
> structurally, an other decision in me, a rending decision as
> the decision of the other. Of the absolutely other in me, of the
> other as the absolute who decides of me in me.[45]

In psychoanalytic terms, this choice is that of the "fundamental fantasy," of the basic frame/matrix which provides the coordinates of the subject's entire universe of meaning: although I am never outside it, although this fantasy is always–already here, and I am always–already thrown into it, I have to presuppose myself as the one who posited it.

Does this mean that the primordial decision forever predetermines the contours of our life? Here enters the "good news" of Christianity: the miracle of faith is that it IS possible to traverse the fantasy, to undo this founding decision, to start one's life all over again, from the zero point – in short, *to change Eternity itself (what we "always–already are")*. Ultimately, the "rebirth" of which Christianity speaks (when one joins the community of believers, one is born again) is the name for such a new Beginning. Against the pagan and/or Gnostic Wisdom which celebrates the (re)discovery of one's true Self – the return to it, the realization of its potentials or whatsoever – Christianity calls upon us to thoroughly reinvent ourselves. Kierkegaard was right: the ultimate choice is the one between the Socratic recollection and the Christian repetition: Christianity enjoins us to REPEAT the founding gesture of the primordial choice. One is almost tempted to put it in the terms of the paraphrase of Marx's "thesis 11": "Philosophers have been teaching us only how to discover (remember) our true Self, but the point is to change it." And THIS Christian legacy, often obfuscated, is today more precious than ever.

From here we should, for the last time, return to Lenin and his critique of "formal freedom": when – to the consternation of liberals – Lenin emphasizes that a Communist revolutionary acknowledges no a priori set of moral rules independent of the revolutionary struggle (like "elementary norms of human decency"), that he views all freedoms and rights with regard to their contribution to this struggle, he is not preaching a Machiavellian moral relativism, but, rather, proposing the revolutionary version of what Kierkegaard referred to as the religious suspension of the ethical. What is this suspension?

Let us take an unexpected example, the final twist of Evelyn Waugh's *Brideshead Revisited*, one of the last great artistic formulations of the logic of the feminine sacrifice: at the novel's end, Julia refuses to marry Ryder (although they have both recently divorced their respective partners for that very reason) as part of what she ironically refers to as her "private deal" with God: although she is corrupt and promiscuous, perhaps there is still a chance for her if she sacrifices what matters most to her, her love for Ryder . . . The perversity of this solution becomes clear the moment we locate it in its proper context: as she makes clear in her final speech to Ryder, Julia is fully aware of her corrupted and promiscuous nature, she is fully aware that, after she drops Ryder, she will have numerous insignificant affairs; however, they don't really count, because they don't condemn her irrevocably in the eyes of God. What would have condemned her is if she were to give privilege to her only true love over her dedication to God, since there should be no competition between supreme goods. Julia thus arrives at the conclusion that the promiscuous corrupted life is for her the only way to retain her chance of mercy in the eyes of God. "God" is thus ultimately the name for the purely negative gesture of meaningless sacrifice, of giving up what matters most to us.

It is here that we encounter the religious suspension of the ethical at its purest: from the ethical standpoint, of course, Julia's choice is meaningless – marriage is infinitely better than extramarital promiscuity; however, from the strictly religious standpoint, to choose marital fidelity would have been the highest treason. Such a tension between the religious and the ethical is, perhaps, what defines modernity: in premodern times, there is literally no place for it to emerge.

In this precise sense, Christianity is, from its very inception, THE religion of modernity: what the Christian notion of the suspension of the Law aims at is precisely this gap between the domain of moral norms and Faith, the unconditional engagement. Bertolt Brecht made the same point in his poem "The Interrogation of the Good":

> Step forward: we hear
> That you are a good man.
>
> You cannot be bought, but the lightning
> Which strikes the house, also
> Cannot be bought.
> You hold to what you said.
> But what did you say?
> You are honest, you say your opinion.
> Which opinion?

You are brave.
Against whom?
You are wise.
For whom?
You do not consider your personal advantages.
Whose advantages do you consider then?
You are a good friend.
Are you also a good friend of the good people?

Hear us then: we know
You are our enemy. This is why we shall
Now put you in front of a wall. But in consideration
of your merits and good qualities
We shall put you in front of a good wall and shoot you
With a good bullet from a good gun and bury you
With a good shovel in the good earth.[46]

Far from cancelling ethics such a suspension is the sine qua non of an authentic unconditional ethical engagement – nowhere is the inherent nullity of the ethics bereft of this suspension clearer than in today's proliferation of the "ethical committees" trying in vain to constrain scientific progress into the straight-jacket of "norms" (how far should we go in biogenetics, etc.). And what is the Christian notion of being "reborn in faith" if not the first full-fledged formulation of such an unconditional subjective engagement on account of which we are ready to suspend the very ethical substance of our being?

Notes

INTRODUCTION

1 Which prolongs, often in a self-critical mood, the analyses of my *The Fragile Absolute. Why Is the Christian Legacy Worth Fighting For?* London: Verso Books 2000.

2 See Michael Hardt and Antonio Negri, *Empire*, Cambridge, MA: Harvard University Press 2000.

ONE AGAINST THE DIGITAL HERESY

1 Harold Bloom, *Omens of Millennium*, London: Fourth Estate 1996, p. 252.

2 Furthermore and along the same lines, is not the obvious solution to the immaculate conception mystery (how the Virgin Mary got pregnant without having sexual intercourse with her husband) that Christ was simply her ILLEGITIMATE son?

3 Zoe Oldenbourg, *Massacre at Montségur*, London: Orion Books 1998, p. 39.

4 See Martin Heidegger, *Zollikoner Seminare*. Herausgegeben von Medard Boss, Frankfurt: Vittorio Klostermann 1987, p. 223–5.

5 Martin Heidegger, *Schelling's Treatise on Human Freedom*, Athens, OH: Ohio University Press 1985, p. 146.

6 See Peter Sloterdijk, *Eurotaoismus*, Frankfurt: Suhrkamp Verlag 1989.

7 In a strictly homologous way, the opposition between globalization and the survival of local traditions is false: globalization directly resuscitates local traditions, it literally thrives on them, which is why the true opposite of globalization is not local traditions, but *universality*. See Chapter IV of Slavoj Žižek, *The Ticklish Subject*, London: Verso Books 1999.

8 In the classic literature, one should mention Emile Zola's *Germinal*, in which his attachment to a rabbit helps the Russian revolutionary

Souvarine to survive – when the rabbit is slaughtered and eaten by mistake, he explodes in an outburst of violent rage.

9 See Gilles Deleuze and Félix Guattari, *Anti-Oedipus: Capitalism and Schizo-phrenia*, Minneapolis, MN: Minnesota University Press 1983.

10 For a further development of this point, see Chapter 3 of Slavoj Žižek, *The Fragile Absolute*.

11 See Jacques Lacan, *Seminar VII: On the Ethics of Psychoanalysis*, New York: Routledge 1992.

12 See Jacques Lacan, *Seminar XX: Encore* (1972/73), New York: Norton 1998.

13 Jacques-Alain Miller, "Paradigms of *Jouissance*," in *Lacanian Ink* 17, New York 2000, p. 33.

14 Ibid., p. 35.

15 Ibid., p. 41.

16 In parallel with Lacan, this idea was also developed by Jean Laplanche in his *New Foundations for Psychoanalysis*, Oxford: Basil Blackwell 1989.

17 See Jacques Lacan, *The Four Fundamental Concepts of Psycho-Analysis*, Harmondsworth: Penguin 1979, p. 256.

18 Miller, op. cit., p. 39.

19 Daniel C. Dennett, *Consciousness Explained*, New York: Little, Brown and Company 1991, p. 410.

20 For a further elaboration of this point, see Slavoj Žižek, *On Love*, London: Routledge 2001.

21 See Ulrich Beck, *Risk Society: Towards a New Modernity*, London: Sage 1992.

22 See Jacques Lacan, *Seminaire, livre XVII: L'envers de la psychanalyse*, Paris: Éditions du Seuil 1996.

23 See Ray Kurzweil, *The Age of Spiritual Machines*, London: Phoenix 1999.

24 See Eric Davis, *TechGnosis*, London: Serpent's Tail 1999.

25 See N. Katherine Hayles, *How We Became Posthuman*, Chicago, IL: The University of Chicago Press 1999.

26 See Hubert Dreyfus, *What Computers Can't Do*, New York: Harper and Row 1979.

27 Hayles, op.cit., p. 5. Where Hayles gets it wrong is in her crude opposition between the liberal self-identical autonomous human subject of the Enlightenment and the posthuman body in which the frontier that separates my autonomous Self from its machinical protheses is constantly permeated, and in which the Self in itself explodes into the famous

"society of minds." The Enlightenment itself not only had a deeply ambiguous relationship towards the mechanical aspect of a human being (recall the motif of l'homme machine in eighteenth-century mechanical materialism); in an even more radical way, one can claim that the Cartesian subject of the Enlightenment, especially in its radicalized version in German Idealism, already IS "post-human," i.e. it has to be strictly opposed to the human person – the Kantian subject of transcendental apperception is a pure void of the negative self-relationship which emerges through the violent gesture of abstracting from all "pathological" content which makes up the wealth of a "human personality."

28 Primo Levi, If This Is a Man / The Truce, London: Abacus 1987, p. 395.
29 Ibid., p. 396.
30 See Hannah Arendt, Eichmann in Jerusalem: A Report on the Banality of Evil, New York: Viking Press 1965.
31 Primo Levi, op. cit., p. 396.
32 Quoted from Julian Young, Heidegger, Philosophy, Nazism, Cambridge: Cambridge University Press 1997, p. 172.
33 Primo Levi, op. cit., p. 393.
34 So what about the "revisionist" argument according to which the Nazi elimination of the racial enemy was just the repetitive displacement on the racial axis of the Soviet Communist elimination of the class enemy? Even if true, the dimension of displacement is crucial, not just a secondary negligible feature: it stands for the shift from the SOCIAL struggle, the admission of the inherently antagonistic character of social life, to the extermination of the NATURALIZED enemy which, from outside, penetrates and threatens the social organism.
35 English translation: Michel Houellebecq, Atomised, London: Heinemann 2000.
36 Hayles, op. cit., p. 8.
37 And, incidentally, with all the focus on the new experiences of pleasure that lie ahead with the development of Virtual Reality, direct neuronal implants, etc., what about new "enhanced" possibilities of TORTURE? Do biogenetics and virtual reality combined open up new and unheard-of horizons of extending our ability to endure pain (through widening our sensory capacity to sustain pain, through inventing new forms of inflicting it) – perhaps, the ultimate Sadean image of an "undead"

victim of the torture who can sustain endless pain without having at his or her disposal the escape into death, also waits to become reality? Perhaps, in a decade or two, our most horrifying cases of torture (for example, what they did to the Chief of Staff of the Dominican Army after the failed coup in which the dictator Trujillo was killed – sewing his eyes together so that he wasn't able to see his torturers, and then for four months slowly cutting off parts of his body in most painful ways, like using blunt scissors to detach his genitals) will appear as naive children's games.

38 Hayles, op. cit., p. 8.

39 Translated by Tom Levine in *October* 55, Winter 1990, p. 48–55.

40 The same holds for today's prospect of virtual reality: the more perfect the digital reproduction, the more "artificial" its effect, in the same way an imperfect black-and-white photo is experienced as more "realistic" than a color photo, although reality is in color.

41 Does not Lacan's reading of "wo es war soll ich werden" involve the temporality of the failed encounter, of not-yet and no-longer, of In-itself and For-itself? The subject is the vanishing mediator between "where it (i.e., what will become a subject) was" (in the state of in-itself, not yet fully realized), and the full symbolic realization in which the subject is already stigmatized into a signifier. Lacan refers here to the Freudian dream of the father who *didn't know he was dead* (and for that reason remained alive): the subject is also only alive insofar as it doesn't know (that he is dead) – the moment he "knows it", assuming symbolic knowledge, he dies (in the signifier which represents him).

42 Maimon Cohen, Director of the Harvey Institute for Human Genetics at the Greater Baltimore Medical Center, quoted in *International Herald Tribune*, 27 June, 2000, p. 8.

43 See Francisco Varela, Evan Thompson and Eleanor Rosch, *The Embodied Mind*, Cambridge, MA: MIT Press 1993.

44 See Steven Pinker, *The Language Instinct*, New York: Harper Books 1995.

45 It is, of course, the work of Daniel Dennett which popularized this version of the "selfless" mind – see Daniel C. Dennett, *Consciousness Explained*, New York: Little, Brown and Company 1991.

46 There is a further proof which points in the same direction: a couple of milliseconds *before* a human subject "freely" decides in a situation of choice, scanners can detect the change in the brain's chemical processes

which indicates that the decision has already been made – even when we make a free decision, our consciousness seems just to register an anterior chemical process . . . The psychoanalytic–Schellingian answer to it is to locate freedom (of choice) at the *unconscious* level: the true acts of freedom are choices/decisions which we make while unaware of it – we never decide (in the present tense); all of a sudden, we just take note of how *we have already decided*.

47 See Ray Kurzweil, op. cit., p. 182.

48 Ibid., p. 183.

49 Ibid., p. 188.

50 Incidentally, the same debilitating deadlock already casts its shadow over the old Aristotelian couple of form and matter: on the one hand, form is universal and matter is conceived of as the principle of individuation; on the other hand, matter in itself is just a formless clay differentiated through the imposition of some determinate form.

51 Martin Heidegger, *Heraclitus Seminar* (with Eugen Fink), Huntington: University of Alabama Press 1979, p. 146.

TWO YOU *SHOULD* GIVE A SHIT!

1 G.W.F. Hegel, *Phenomenology of Spirit*, Oxford: Oxford University Press 1977, p. 421–24.

2 Ibid., p. 421.

3 Ibid., p. 423.

4 Ibid., p. 423.

5 Ibid., p. 423.

6 See Dominique Laporte, *History of Shit*, Cambridge, MA: The MIT Press 2000.

7 In the Ancient Greek theatre, there was a hole in the middle of the large stone seats in the first rows – members of the privileged classes were thus able to undergo a *double* catharsis, the spiritual purification of cleansing their soul of bad emotions, as well as the bodily purification of the smelly excrement.

8 Otto Weininger, *Ueber die letzten Dinge*, München: Matthes und Seitz Verlag 1997, p. 187.

9 Ibid., p. 188.

10 Quoted from Orville Schell, *Virtual Tibet*, New York: Henry Holt and Company 2000, p. 80.

11 Ibid., p. 202.

12 Ibid., p. 191.

13 Ibid., p. 191.

14 Ibid., p. 230.

15 William McGovern in Schell, op. cit., p. 230.

16 Is not the obvious thing for an analyst to root Envy in the infamous penis envy? Rather than succumbing to this temptation, one should emphasize that envy is ultimately the envy of the Other's *jouissance*. My affluent business-oriented colleagues always marvel at how much work I put into theory and, comparatively, how little I earn; although their marvel is usually expressed in terms of aggressive scorn ("How stupid you are to deal with theory!"). What obviously lurks behind this is envy: the idea that, since I am not doing it for money (or power), and since they do not get the reason I am doing it, there must be some strange *jouissance*, some satisfaction in theory accessible only to me, out of reach to them . . .

17 The mention of le Carré is far from accidental here: in his great (early) spy novels, he repeatedly stages the same fundamental scenario of the interconnection of love and betrayal, i.e. of how, far from the two terms being simply opposed, betraying someone serves as the ultimate proof of loving him/her. Is betrayal for the sake of love not the ultimate form of sacrifice?

18 This also enables us to answer Dominick la Capra's reproach according to which, the Lacanian notion of lack conflates two levels that have to be kept apart: the purely formal "ontological" lack constitutive of the symbolic order as such, and the particular traumatic experiences (exemplarily: Holocaust) which could also NOT have occurred – particular historical catastrophes like the Holocaust thus seem to be "legitimized" as directly grounded in the fundamental trauma that pertains to human existence. (See Dominick la Capra, "Trauma, Absence, Loss," *Critical Inquiry*, Volume 25, Number 4 (Summer 1999), pp. 696–727.) Against this misunderstanding, one should emphasize that the quasi-transcendental lack and particular traumas are linked in a negative way: far from being just the last link in the continuous chain of traumatic encounters that reaches back to the "symbolic castration," catastrophes like the Holocaust are contingent (and, as such, avoidable) events which occur as the final result of

the endeavors to OBFUSCATE the quasi-transcendental constitutive lack.

19 Madame de Lafayette, *The Princesse de Clèves*, Harmondsworth: Penguin Books 1978, p. 170.
20 Ibid., p. 38.
21 Jacques Lacan, *Écrits: A Selection*, New York: Norton 1977, p. 319.
22 Ibid., p. 322.
23 Regina Barecca, "Introduction" to Henry James, *The Portrait of a Lady*, New York: Signet Classic 1995, p. xiii.
24 The first to accomplish a homologous gesture was Medea as anti-Antigone: she first kills her brother (her closest family relative), thus cutting off her roots radically, rendering impossible any return, putting all her bets on the marriage with Jason; after betraying everyone close to her FOR Jason and then being betrayed BY Jason himself, there is nothing left to her, she finds herself in the void – the void of self-relating negativity, of the "negation of negation," that is subjectivity itself. So it's time to reassert Medea against Antigone: Medea or Antigone, that's the ultimate choice today. In other words, how are we to fight power? Through the fidelity to the old organic Mores threatened by Power, or by out-violencing Power itself? Two versions of femininity: Antigone can still be read as standing for particular family roots against the universality of the public space of State Power; Medea, on the contrary, out-universalizes universal Power itself.
25 Gilles Deleuze, *L'image-mouvement*, Paris: Éditions de Minuit 1983, p. 234–6.
26 The asymmetry of the apparently symmetrical reversals is crucial to explain the mechanisms of ideological genesis; let us take the case of agreement/disagreement. First, we simply agree; then, we pass to disagreement, which means that we "disagree to agree"; however, if we reverse "disagree to agree" into "agree to disagree," we get a more complex double-level notion: to "agree to disagree" is not simply to agree in the same way "disagree to agree" is simply to disagree, but to establish a common symbolic pact which allows us to communicate "peacefully" our disagreement itself. In a sense, the symbolic pact/agreement AS SUCH is always minimally a gesture of "agreeing to disagree," of accepting a common ground that prevents the disagreement from exploding into a deadly violence.

27 I borrowed this notion from Alenka Zupancic.

28 Christa Wolf, *The Quest for Christa T.*, New York: Farrar, Straus & Giroux 1970, p. 24.

29 However, it was Greene himself who, in the novel, condensed into the figure of heroine Sarah TWO of his real-life lovers: as to the circumstances of the affair (London during the Nazi bombing, etc.), the model is Dorothy Glover, a small, poor, stocky air-raid shelter custodian, Greene's lover in the early 1940s; the model of physical beauty and passionate sexual promiscuity is the very rich Lady Catherine Walston. It is thus as if, in the passage from the novel to the film, the very displacement was again displaced.

30 Martin Heidegger, *Zollikoner Seminare*, Frankfurt: Vittorio Klostermann 1987, p. 260.

31 For a more detailed elaboration of this key feature, see Chapter 1 of Slavoj Žižek, *Did Somebody Say Totalitarianism?*, London: Verso Books 2001, where I rely on Jean Laplanche's exemplary account in his *Essays on Otherness*, London: Routledge 1999.

32 I am borrowing this formula of love as the "accessible transcendence" from Alenka Zupancic, to whom this whole passage is deeply indebted.

33 Franz Kafka, *Wedding Preparations in the Country and Other Stories*, Harmondsworth: Penguin 1978, p. 173–74.

34 Of course, it's not the physical appearance of the vagina which matters: what matters is that this vagina belongs to the beloved person. In other words, and to indulge in a rather tasteless mental experiment: if I were to discover that the identical-looking vagina belonged to a different person (or that the person that I loved had a different vagina), then this same vagina would no longer exert the unconditional fascination. What this means is that drive and desire are nonetheless inherently interwoven: not only does desire always rely on some partial drives which provide its "stuff"; drives also function only insofar as they refer to the subject whose desire I desire.

35 See Bernard Baas, *De la Chose à l'objet*, Leuven: Pieters 1998, especially pp. 71–8.

36 Jacques Lacan, *Écrits*, Paris: Editions du Seuil 1966, p. 818.

37 These speculations of Lacan are clearly indebted to his friend Maurice Merleau-Ponty's explorations, posthumously collected in *Le visible et l'invisible*, Paris: Gallimard 1964. Lacan refers to Merleau-Ponty especially in

Part II of his *Four Fundamental Concepts of Psycho-Analysis*, New York: Norton 1979.

38 See the Epilogue of Eric Santner, *On the Psychotheology of Everyday Life*, Chicago, IL: University of Chicago Press 2001.

39 See Bernard Bass, *Le désir pur*, Leuven: Peeters 1992.

40 See Jacques Lacan, *Le séminaire, livre VII: L'éthique de la psychanalyse*, Paris: Éditions du Seuil 1986, p. 133.

41 See, for example, Jacques Lacan, "Desire and the interpretation of desire in *Hamlet*," in *Literature and Psychoanalysis*, ed. by Shoshana Felman, Baltimore, MD: Johns Hopkins University Press 1980, p. 15.

42 See Jonathan Lear, *Happiness, Death, and the Remainder of Life*, Cambridge, MA: Harvard University Press 2000.

43 For this idea, see Eric Santner's outstanding *On the Psychotheology of Everyday Life*, Chicago, IL: University of Chicago Press 2001.

THREE "FATHER, WHY DID YOU FORSAKE ME?"

1 Furthermore, does the triad of Deleuze/Derrida/Lacan also not display a clear religious connotation: the pagan Deleuze, the Jewish Derrida, and the Christian Lacan?

2 Is it not that, ultimately, philosophy AS SUCH begins with Kant, with his transcendental turn? Is it not that the entire previous philosophy can be understood properly (not as the simple description of the "entire universe," of the totality of beings, but as the description of the horizon within which entities disclose themselves to a finite human being) only if read "anachronistically," from the standpoint opened up by Kant? Is it not that it was Kant who also opened up the field within which Heidegger himself was able to formulate the notion of *Dasein* as the place in which beings appear within a historically determined/destined horizon of meaning?

3 See Philippe Lacou-Labarthe, *La Fiction du politique*, Paris: Christian Bourgeois 1987.

4 Martin Heidegger, *An Introduction to Metaphysics*, New Haven, CT: Yale University Press 1959, p. 77.

5 See Jacques Lacan, *Le séminaire, livre VIII: Le Transfert*, Paris: Éditions du Seuil 1986.

6 See Octave Mannoni, "Je sais bien, mais quand même . . . ," in *Clefs pour l'imaginaire*, Paris: Éditions du Seuil 1968.

7 Franz Kafka, *The Trial*, Harmondsworth: Penguin Books 1985, p. 238–9.

8 Ibid., p. 240.

9 Ibid., p. 241.

10 One of the few points where pagan mythology comes close to this Kafkaesque procedure is, in the Grail legend, the famous mistake of Parsifal during his first encounter with the ailing Fisher King: he fails simply because he does not directly ASK the King the question: "What is wrong with you?"

11 For a detailed deployment of the notion of Event, see Alain Badiou, *L'être et l'évènement*, Paris: Éditions du Seuil 1989, as well as Alain Badiou, *Ethics*, London: Verso Books 2000.

12 And, interestingly, when, in my account of Badiou (see Chapter 3 of *The Ticklish Subject*), I point out the religious paradigm of his notion of the Event of Truth, many a critic of Badiou referred to me approvingly, as if I meant this as a criticism of Badiou. That such is not the case is amply proved by my ensuing book, *The Fragile Absolute*.

13 Hannah Arendt, "What Is Freedom?," in *Between Past and Future*, New York: Penguin Books 1968, p. 151.

14 Ibid., p. 165.

15 Wendy Brown, *States of Injury*, Princeton, NJ: Princeton University Press 1995, p. 14. Another strange bedfellow of Badiou is none other than Heidegger: is Badiou's attitude towards the differences within the positive order of Being, of "servicing the goods" (ultimately, he dismisses the differences between liberal democracy and the variants of direct dictatorship as of no serious interest, since they all lack the dimension of the Event of Truth) not strictly correlative to Heidegger's assertion that liberalism, Nazism and Communism are metaphysically the same, so that – since they all partake in the epochal nihilism of the technological Will-to-Power, and thus obliterate the only dimension that really matters, that of the thought of Being – the difference between democracy and Nazism is ultimately irrelevant?

16 V.I. Lenin, "Political Report of the Central Committee of the R.C.P. (B.)," March 27, 1922, in *Collected Works*, Moscow: Progress 1965, Volume 33, p. 283.

17 See Claude Lefort, *Democracy and Political Theory*, Minneapolis, MN: Minnesota University Press 1988.

18 To put it in Alain Badiou's terms of the opposition of Being and Event

(see, again, his *L'être et l'évènement*), the rise of the term "Really Existing Socialism" signalled the final and full reinscription of the Communist regimes into the positive order of Being: even the minimal utopian potential still discernible in the wildest Stalinist mobilization and, later, in the Khruschevian "thaw," definitely disappeared.

19 See Ulrich Beck, *Risk Society: Towards a New Modernity*, London: Sage 1992.

20 See Jean-Leon Beauvois, *Traité de la servitude liberale. Analyse de la soumission*, Paris: Dunod 1994.

21 See Chapters 2 and 3 of Susan Buck-Morss, *Dreamworld and Catastrophe*, Cambridge, MA: MIT Press 2000.

22 *Hegel's Philosophy of Mind*, Oxford: Clarendon Press 1971, p. 315.

23 This maxim was formulated by the Hungarian Jesuit Hevenesi in 1705; for its Lacanian reading, see Louis Beirnaert, *Aux frontières de l'acte analytique. La Bible, Saint Ignace, Freud et Lacan*, Paris: Éditions du Seuil 1987, p. 219–27.

24 The reflections which follow are deeply indebted to Eric Santner's outstanding *On the Psychotheology of Everyday Life. Reflections on Freud and Rosenzweig*, Chicago, IL: University of Chicago Press 2001.

25 At the same time, however, one should emphasize the *opposite* movement: does not Christianity also involve the expectation of Christ's *second* coming, i.e. the teleological stance oriented towards the future of the Last Judgement, when all symbolic accounts will be settled? It is here that the reference to Judaism should serve as the corrective: in a way, Christ's death already IS the fulfillment, there is nothing to follow.

26 Recall the bizarre accident in New York Beth Israel hospital on September 7 1999: after performing a Caesarian section on a patient, Dr. Alan Zarkin carved his initial into her abdomen – proud of his perfect work, he wanted to leave a kind of mark on the body, like the artist's signature.

27 See Jacques Rancière, *La mésentente*, Paris: Galilée 1995.

28 Within the Jewish tradition itself, this iconoclastic prohibition reverberates in the motif of Golem, the giant created by men who, by endeavoring to imitate God's life-giving creativity, created a monster – the second Commandment does not aim primarily at painting, but, more generally, at the human imitation of the divine creativity.

29 See Philippe Lacoue-Labarthe, *Musica Ficta*, Stanford, CA: Stanford University Press 1994.

30 Similar is the case of the Nazi anti-Semitism: the standard

(pseudo)explanation of the growing acceptance of the Nazi ideology in the Germany of the 1920s is that the Nazis were deftly manipulating ordinary middle-class people's fears and anxieties generated by the economic crisis and rapid social change. The problem with this explanation is that it overlooks the self-referential circularity at work here: yes, the Nazis certainly did deftly manipulate fears and anxieties – however, far from being simple pre-ideological facts, *these fears and anxieties were already the product of a certain ideological perspective*. In other words, the Nazi ideology itself (co)generated "anxieties and fears" against which it then proposed itself as a solution.

31 Along these lines, one is tempted to claim that Judaism is caught in the paradox of prohibiting what is already in itself impossible: if one CANNOT render God through images, why PROHIBIT images? To claim that, by making images of Him, we do not show a proper respect for Him, is all too simple, since, as we know from psychoanalysis, respect is ultimately the respect for the Other's weakness – to treat someone with respect means that one maintains a proper distance towards him, avoiding acts which, if accomplished, would unmask his stance as an imposture. Say, when a father boasts to his son that he could run fast, the respectful thing to do is NOT to defy him to do it, since this would reveal his impotence . . . In other words, the idea that iconoclasm expresses the respect for the divine Other makes sense only as the indication of some Other's impotence or limitation.

32 In the contemporary art enterprise, the curator seems to play a role uncannily similar to that of Christ: is he not also a kind of "vanishing mediator" between the Artist-Creator ("God") and the community of the public ("believers")? This new role of the curator in the last decades hinges on two interconnected processes. On the one hand, works of art themselves have lost their innocence: an artist no longer just spontaneously creates and leaves to the other the interpretation of what he does – the reference to the future (theoretical) interpretation is already part of his immediate artistic production, so that the temporal loop is closed, and the author's work is a kind of preemptive strike, dialoguing with, responding in advance to, its future imagined interpretations. These potential interpretations are embodied in the figure of the Curator; he is the transferential subject for the artists themselves – he does not simply collect preexisting works, these works are already

created with the Curator in view, their ideal interpreter (more and more, he even directly solicits or employs artists to execute his vision). On the other hand, it is a fact that, at today's large exhibitions, the broad public no longer has the time to "slow down" and really immerse itself in the vast collection of works – the problem here is not so much that they do not get what is going on, that they need some explanation, but that today's artworks can no longer be directly experienced with the intensity that bears witness to a strong impact of the work itself. So, for this broad public, the Curator is not so much the interpreter as the ideal passive viewer who was still able to "slow down," to take time and experience all the works as a passive viewer. The public then plays the intellectually well-versed spectators who, while having neither the time nor the ability to fully immerse themselves into the proper passive experience of the work, exchange witty quasi-theoretical remarks or opinions, leaving the direct experience of the work to the Curator as the Subject Supposed to Experience the work of art.

33 Immanuel Kant, *Critique of Pure Reason*, London: Everyman's Library 1988, p. 12.

34 For a good account of the false translations of this key passage, see Gerard Guest, *La Tournure de l'évènement*, Berlin: Duncker und Humboldt 1994.

35 See Eric Santner, "Traumatic Revelations: Freud's Moses and the Origins of Anti-Semitism," in Renata Salecl ed., *Sexuation*, Durham, NC: Duke University Press 2000.

36 See Jacques Lacan, *Écrits*, Paris: Éditions du Seuil 1966, p. 768–72.

37 I rely here again on Bernard Baas's excellent *De la Chose à l'objet*.

38 See Jacques-Alain Miller, "Théorie du caprice," in *Quarto* 71, Bruxelles 2000, pp. 6–12.

39 This distinction between enunciated and enunciation also accounts for the basic lesson of the so-called capitalist Protestant ethic: why greed has to turn into its apparent opposite, into ascetism, the prohibition to consume and enjoy what we amass. Greed at the level of the "enunciated" – as the explicit goal of our activity – can only be properly practised if our innermost subjective attitude is that of a thorough ascetism. (The same point can be made also in terms of potentiality and actuality: in order fully to enjoy himself, a greedy subject has to postpone indefinitely the full consumption of what he is amassing, relating

to this moment as a permanent possibility, a promise that will never
realize itself.)

40 Is, then, Islam a solution? Does Islam not perceive this deadlock of both
religions? Does it, consequently, not endeavor to accomplish a kind of
"synthesis" of the two? Perhaps, although I am not in a position to
pass a competent judgement on it, since, from MY (Judeo–Christian)
perspective, it appears as if, in this attempted synthesis, Islam ends up
with the worst of both worlds. That is to say, the common reproach
of Christians to Jews is that their religion is that of a cruel superego,
while the common reproach of Jews to Christians is that, unable to
endure in pure monotheism, they regress to a mythical narrative (of
Christ's martyrdom, etc.) and is it not that, in Islam, we find BOTH,
narrative and superego?

41 See Herbert Schnädelbach, "Der Fluch des Christentums," *Die Zeit* 20,
11 Mai 2000, pp. 41–2.

42 One should not forget that the notion of Mercy is strictly correlative to
that of Sovereignty: only the bearer of sovereign power can dispense
mercy.

43 Is there, then, a dimension BEYOND the enigma of the Other's desire?
What if the ultimate horizon of our experience is NOT the abyss of the
Other's desire? The danger here is, of course, to avoid "regressing" to
the pagan experience of *nirvana* or some other version of cosmic
Gelassenheit.

44 F.W.J. von Schelling, *Ages of the World*, Ann Arbor, MI: The University of
Michigan Press 1997, pp. 181–2. See also Chapter 1 of Slavoj Žižek, *The
Indivisible Remainder*, London: Verso Books 1997.

45 Jacques Derrida, *Adieu à Emmanuel Levinas*, Paris: Galilée 1997, p. 87.

46 Bertolt Brecht, "Verhör des Guten," (my translation) in *Werke: Band 18,
Prosa 3*, Frankfurt am Main: Suhrkamp Verlag 1995, p. 502–3.

Index

Adam's Fall 7–9, 105, 146
addiction 102–3
Adorno, Theodor 11, 44–5, 87–9
alien invasion 20, 61–2, 79, 131
Althusser, Louis 138
anal objects 56–68
Ancient Egypt 56–9, 145
anthropomorphism 129–31
Antigone 19, 30, 92, 137
anti-Semitism 38–9, 83
anxiety 73–4
Arendt, Hannah 38, 112–13
Aristotle 100, 101, 104
artificers 56–9
authenticity 44–5
authoritarianism 118–20

Baas, Bernard 95, 97–8
Badiou, Alain 112–13, 125–6, 144
Bataille, Laurence 30
Beauvois, Jean-Léon 117, 118–20
Beck, Ulrich 27, 116
belief 109–13
body 33–6, 54–5, 56–9
Boss, Medard 10, 86
Brecht, Bertolt 4, 150–1

Buddhism 12, 63–8
Bunuel, Luis 60

Camus, Albert 102
capitalism 12–21, 31–2
Carrey, Jim 62–3
castration, symbolic 72–4
Cathars 7–8
Chaplin, Charlie 79, 90
Charles I (King of England) 119
choice 28, 36, 115–23, 148–9
Claudel, Paul 78, 92
Clinton, President Bill 115
cognitivists 12, 25–6
collective organizations 4, 16
comedy 90–2
communication 26–7, 43, 52–3
Communism 4, 18–19, 36, 39, 81,
    139, 149
community 127–9
Conservatism 3–5, 40
consumption 20–1, 30
Cooper, Gary 70
Copernicus 134–5
Curzon, Lord 66
cyberspace 25–6, 33–4, 48–55

Dasein (being-there) 9, 34, 106–7
death (bereavement) 13–14
death drive 100, 104
decision 147–8
deconstructionists 2, 25–6, 34, 83
Deleuze, Gilles 18, 79
Dennett, Daniel 25
Derrida, Jacques 18, 20, 148
Descartes, René 34–5, 133, 135
desire 74–8, 91–2
desublimation 39–41, 89–90
dialectics, negative 88–9
digital revolution 32, 33–55
domination 17, 35, 39
Dreyfus, Hubert 106
drives 10, 63, 91, 93–8, 100, 104
Durkheim, Emile 102

ego-psychology 33, 134–5
Eisenstein, Sergi 123
embodiment 51–2
Engels, Friedrich 2, 142
enlightenment 11, 54
entities 9–11, 33, 42
ethics 1–2, 45, 84, 101, 139–40, 150
Evil 7, 62, 133, 146
exile 127–37

faith 109–13, 148–51
Fascism 38–9
feminine renunciation 68–89
feminization 33
fetishism 13–15, 99–100, 125–6
Foucault, Michel 40

freedom 112–27, 149
Freud, Sigmund 2–3, 11, 15, 36–7, 46, 55, 63, 81–2, 86–7, 91, 93, 100–1, 104, 130, 134–5, 144, 145
Fukuyama, Francis 111
fundamentalism 68–9

gadgets 20–2, 31
genetic technology 34–50
globalization 2, 4–5, 18, 26, 32, 36, 52
Gnosticism 6–15, 33–4, 54–5, 141, 148
Goethe, Johann Wolfgang von 77
Greene, Graham 85–6
Groys, Boris 90
Guattari, Félix 18
guilt 17–18, 127

Habermas, Jürgen 27, 89
Hayles, Katherine 35, 43
Hegel, G.W.F. 16, 31, 41, 47, 56–8, 60, 89, 115, 125, 126, 129, 132, 133, 135, 140, 145
Heidegger, Martin 8–11, 34–5, 38–9, 53, 86–7, 106–9
Heraclitus 96–7
Herman, Mark 85
Hitchcock, Alfred 80
Hobbes, Thomas 136
Hölderlin, J.C.F. 96
Holocaust, the 17–18, 36–9
Horkheimer, Max 11
Houellebecq, Michel 39, 40
humanism 11, 36
hysteria 45, 73–4, 84–5, 93

iconoclasm 127–37
individualism 24–5
industrialization 123–4
information technology 33–48
Inner Self 59–60
Irigaray, Luce 128
IRS (imaginary, real, symbolic)
    triad 78, 82, 99

Jakobson, Roman 102
James, Henry 78
Jordan, Neil 86
Judaism 89, 91, 106, 109–12,
    126–37
Judeo–Christian legacy 6, 12, 47,
    111, 126–9, 132, 135–40
Jung, Carl 2–3

Kafka, Franz 64, 92–3, 104,
    110–11
Kant, Immanuel 37, 49, 68, 80, 87,
    89, 91, 94, 95–7, 107, 119, 124,
    133–5, 138–40
Kierkegaard, Søren A. 45, 77, 105,
    148, 149
Kipling, Rudyard 4
Knowledge 9, 37–8
Kusturica, Emir 28

la Boétie 117
Lacan, Jacques 2–3, 11, 17, 19–33,
    37–8, 41, 44, 59, 63, 69–71, 74,
    76–8, 81–4, 87–9, 92, 93, 95–9,
    100–1, 108, 109, 120, 135,
    137–8, 144
Lacoue-Labarthe, Philippe 108
Lafayette, Madame de 74–8

language 27, 43, 47–8, 53, 55
Laplanche 100
Lear, Jonathan 100–1, 104
Leary, Timothy 53
Lefort, Claude 114
Leibniz, Gottfried 26, 52
Lenin, Vladimir Ilyich 2–4, 81, 84,
    113–27, 142, 149
Levi, Primo 37–9
Lewis, Jerry 62
liberalism 3–4, 113, 118–21
Lichtung (clearing) 10–11, 35
Lodge, David 25
Lorenz, Konrad 36
love 39–41, 84, 90, 143, 146–7
Lubitsch, Ernst 79, 90

McGovern, William 67
machines, intelligent 42–3
Mannoni, Octave 109
Marx, Karl 2–3, 8–9, 12–19, 21,
    36, 99, 113, 129, 142
masks 62
Maupassant, Guy de 20
Medusa 20
mercy 142–51
metaphysics 83
Meyerhold, V.E. 123
Miller, Jacques-Alain 19, 23, 27, 29,
    32, 33, 103
miracles 86
monadology 26, 52
money 17, 99–100
myths 11–12

nanobots 50
Nazism 38–9, 124

neural implants 49–51
New Age thought 12, 32, 34, 36
Nietzsche, Friedrich Wilhelm 36–7, 105, 125
norms 61, 151

objectivity 88–9, 114
Oedipus 16, 19, 33, 57–8, 92
Order 126–7
Oriental thought 10–11
Other 23–4, 29, 47, 53, 59, 69–73, 84, 107–9, 127–37, 146–7

Pascal, Blaise 16, 33
philosophy 11, 109, 125
physics 10, 22
Pinker, Steve 47
Plato 11, 96
pleasure principle 76–7
Poe, E.A. 20
politics 2–3, 113, 126
pornography 54
postindustrial society 11, 32
postmodernism 11–12, 32, 39–40, 81, 116, 124
productivity 18–19
psychoanalysis 15–18, 24, 29, 33, 46, 47, 55, 69–70, 74, 83–4, 104, 148
psychology 46, 116–17

racism 32
radical Left 1–2, 4
Rancière, Jacques 128
Reality 14, 80–84, 87–9

reflexive determination 16, 66, 132, 135–6
reflexivity 27–8, 41, 102
revolutionary process 17–18, 41–2, 84
risk society 116
Rorty, Richard 27, 28, 106

sacrifice 68–89, 140–1
Sade, Marquis de 138–40
Saint Augustine 132
Saint Francis 8
Saint Paul 2–3, 143–4
Saint Thomas 20
Santner, Eric 96, 137
Schelling, F.W.J. 10, 96, 140, 147
Schnädelbach, Herbert 142–3
Scott, Ridley 20, 61–2, 131
Sein (being) 9, 107–8
Self 26, 33, 48–55, 59
sexual difference 40, 42–6
sexuality 15, 20–4, 31, 33, 40–2, 93–5
Sholder, Jack 61
Shute, Nevil 14–15
Socialism 4, 39, 81, 114–15, 120–1, 123–4
Socrates 101, 108–9, 148
Solzhenytsin, Alexander 61
Sorokin, Vladimir 60–1
Spinoza, Baruch 106
spirituality 42, 53–5
Stalin, Joseph 39, 81, 123–4, 139, 142
subjectivity 45, 49, 56–8
sublimation 41, 89–90
suicide 102–3

superego 74, 141, 144–5
symbolic acts 84–5
symbolic order 30–1, 43–4
Szwarc, Jeannot 71

Taoism 12
technology 10, 11–12, 20–1, 34–48
theft 70–1
Thing, the 19–20, 29, 31, 69, 97–8, 100, 131
Third Way 3, 32, 115
Tibet 63–8, 69
totalitarianism 118–20
transcendental illusion 68, 80, 87–8, 95, 107
trauma 36–8, 46–8, 86–7
truth 4–5, 63, 144
Turin Shroud 98–9

Turing, Alan 42–3
Tvardovsky, Konstantin 61

understanding 37–8
universalism 143–4
utility fog 50
utopianism 81

Varela, Francisco 47
Virtual Reality 33–4, 42, 50–3

Wachowski brothers 53
Waugh, Evelyn 149–50
Weber, Max 13
Weininger, Otto 59
Western Buddhism 12–13, 15, 26
Wittgenstein, Ludwig 128

Younghusband, Francis 66

THINKING IN ACTION – order more now

Available from all good bookshops

Credit card orders can be made on our **Customer Hotlines**:
UK/RoW: + (0) 8700 768 853
US/Canada: (1) 800 634 7064

Or buy online at: www.routledge.com

Routledge
Taylor & Francis Group

TITLE	AUTHOR	ISBN	BIND	PRICES UK	US	CANADA
On Belief	Slavoj Zizek	0415255325	PB	£8.99	$14.95	$19.95
On Cosmopolitanism and Forgiveness	Jacques Derrida	0415227127	PB	£8.99	$14.95	$19.95
On Film	Stephen Mulhall	0415247969	PB	£8.99	$14.95	$19.95
On Being Authentic	Charles Guignon	0415261236	PB	£8.99	$14.95	$19.95
On Humour	Simon Critchley	0415251214	PB	£8.99	$14.95	$19.95
On Immigration and Refugees	Sir Michael Dummett	0415227089	PB	£8.99	$14.95	$19.95
On Anxiety	Renata Salecl	0415312760	PB	£8.99	$14.95	$19.95
On Literature	Hillis Miller	0415261252	PB	£8.99	$14.95	$19.95
On Religion	John D Caputo	041523333X	PB	£8.99	$14.95	$19.95
On Humanism	Richard Norman	0415305233	PB	£8.99	$14.95	$19.95
On Science	Brian Ridley	0415249805	PB	£8.99	$14.95	$19.95
On Stories	Richard Kearney	0415247985	PB	£8.99	$14.95	$19.95
On Personality	Peter Goldie	0415305144	PB	£8.99	$14.95	$19.95
On the Internet	Hubert Dreyfus	0415228077	PB	£8.99	$14.95	$19.95
On Evil	Adam Morton	0415305195	PB	£8.99	$14.95	$19.95
On the Meaning of Life	John Cottingham	0415248000	PB	£8.99	$14.95	$19.95
On Cloning	John Harris	0415317002	PB	£8.99	$14.95	$19.95

Contact our **Customer Hotlines** for details of postage
and packing charges where applicable.
All prices are subject to change
without notification.

...Big ideas to fit in your pocket